A Lightning Slinger's Tales of the Rails

Dr. Vera E. Williams, Ph.D.

Stories compiled and edited by
Jill S. Flateland

Copyright © 2011 by Vera E. Williams

All rights reserved, including the right to reproduce this book or portions thereof in any form whatsoever. For information address Jill S. Flateland, 11350 W. 72nd Place, Arvada, CO.

Mystery Book Nook Publishing

ISBN-10: 09829077-4-5

EAN-13: 97809829077-4-0

Cover illustration by Byron B. Flateland

First printing: August 2011

Second printing, August, 2015

Third printing, July, 2016

Printed in the United States of America

10 9 8 7 6 5 4 3 2 1

Second Edition

Other publications written by Dr. Vera E. Williams, Ph.D. and Vivian V. Lund, M.S. Ed.:

Private Fred W. Barber, Company G, 7th Wisconsin Infantry (Sept 16, 1851 – May 11, 1865), 1988

History of Hawthorne, Wisconsin, 2006

Jakob August and Hilda Sophia Johnson Wattman Family, 2006

Lloyd Lyle and Ethel Elvira Wattman Williams Family, 2008

James Anthony and Vivian Vendela Williams Lund Family, 2011

Dr. Vera E. Williams, Ph.D.:

A Lightning Slinger's Tales of the Rails, 1st edition, 2012

A Lightning Slinger's Tales of the Rails, 2nd edition, 2015

A Lightning Slinger's Tales of the Rails, 3rd edition, 2016

Dedication

This novel is dedicated to my father, Lloyd Lyle Williams, brother, Lyle Chauncey Williams, and step-father, Axel W. Nordholm, all of whom worked for a railroad and had a great deal of influence on my life. My mother, Ethel Elvira Wattman Williams, kept me on task, as she was the chief dispatcher of our family.

If love and laughter help one to live longer, I must thank my two special sisters, Vivian Vendela Williams Lund and Doris Hilda Williams Gezzer. We have spent some wonderful times together.

Vera, Vivian (back row),
Lyle and Doris Williams – 1946

Introduction

An article by Jo Zorr in the March 15, 1987, issue of *Oshkosh Northwestern Newspaper* wrote, "Dr. Vera E. Williams is well known as the train-loving professor of health, physical education and recreation at the University of Wisconsin–Oshkosh. Her devotion to people, athletics, teaching, and railroading has kept her life humming along and on track."

Vowing that she'll wear out before she rusts out, Vera adds, "I was fortunate that my parents believed that girls, as well as boys, should have equal opportunities and training in any type of employment. Thus, I lived the life of a railroader since birth. Now that I've retired, I'm sharing my vast experience, so the youth of today can understand the life of railroading."

Tales of the Rails shares true stories. I hope you enjoy the book.

Dr. Vera E. Williams, Ph.D.

Vera's Office – Memories of Days Gone By

Gratitude

My brother, Lyle Chauncey Williams, was only 16 years old when our father died, and he became the man of the house. Money was scarce, so he went to work sweeping out grain elevators after school.

Mother refused to let Lyle quit school, so he followed Father's footsteps and went to night school to learn telegraphy. He got a job working on the extra board for the Soo Line Railroad. Lyle graduated from East High School in 1941 and after some experience, landed a job at MJ Tower in Superior as a Telegrapher.

On August 26, 1948, he married Rosemary Esther Martin. Together, they raised a rambunctious family of five. Lyle worked 44 years on the Soo Line and retired on February 28, 1986.

Lyle C. Williams Retirement From Soo Line Railroad, 1986

His oldest daughter, Jill Suzanne Williams Flateland, recalls living above the depot for the first 17 years of her life. "It was a unique experience, and I've never regretted it to this day."

Jill compiled my numerous notes, memoirs, and photos to create this history so it won't be lost to the future. At times, she filled in the narrative gaps. Without her help, this book would have taken longer to complete.

Jill S. Williams Flateland

After 36 years, Jill retired from her nurse executive position. She has published several articles on health care, created 26 audio/video courses for continuing education and more than 100 clinical paths in 21 volumes, used throughout the U.S., Japan, Europe, and Australia.

Jill says, "When I'm not researching family history with my two aunts, Vivian and Vera, I write fiction, but railroad will always be in my blood. Like Aunt Vera, I miss the old steam engines chugging down the track followed by the red caboose."

Special thanks to my nieces, Barbara Jean Gezzer Hoffer and Cindy Lea Williams McKinley, who reviewed and edited this book, more than once, and gave terrific feedback.

Jill's husband, Byron Flateland, created the cover to add the finishing touch to this book.

Acknowledgements

I'm grateful for Loren Sloan's help in reviewing and revising this book to assure accuracy. I can't think of anyone better qualified. Loren worked his way up the organization starting as a laborer on the section crew, a telegrapher, depot agent, interlocking leverman, telegrapher-clerk, train dispatcher, and retired as yardmaster.

Loren Sloan

Loren started his railroad career in the spring of 1945. He joined a large wartime crew working for the Soo Line out of Gordon, Wisconsin.

In 1947, he took a railroad telegraphy course during vocational school and joined the Great Northern Railroad. Then he joined the Chicago, St. Paul, Minneapolis, and Omaha Railroad, working at several stations throughout Wisconsin and Minnesota.

His last 18 years brought him back to the Soo Line, where he worked as yardmaster at Stinson yard in Superior, Wisconsin. At that time, it was a very busy terminal operation. The yard office had nearly 500 telegraphers, clerks, and yardmasters, who worked around the clock, seven days a week. Loren retired in 1986. He writes:

"The days have passed when communications depend on the telegrapher and the Morse code. Oh, but those were good days. I hold fond memories as I can still imagine hearing the clicking of the sounders calling our stations. I'd hurry to the telegraph desk and plug into the jack box to get an active wire funneled into the resonator. Then, I'd pull that movable resonator arm next to my ear and sat down to the instrument to answer with our call letters, and prepared to copy on the 'Mill.'"

For those who don't quite understand railroad lingo, the mill, meant taking the message on a typewriter.

Table of Contents

The Big Event 1
Williams Family 4
Hawthorne, Wisconsin 16
Vera's Destiny 30
Great Depression 32
West Duluth, Minnesota 50
Central Avenue, Superior, WI 53
Ironton, Minnesota 57
Motley, Minnesota 61
Moose Lake, Minnesota 68
Wrenshall, Minnesota 70
Carlton, Minnesota 72
Rush City, Minnesota 74
DU at Duluth, Minnesota 75
Poplar, Wisconsin 78
Cloquet, Minnesota 80
Brule, Wisconsin 82
Cromwell, Minnesota 84
Aitkin, Minnesota 88
White Bear Lake, Minnesota 90
Brainerd, Minnesota 92
Hinckley, Minnesota 94
Iron River, Wisconsin 106
Women on the Railroad 110
By Gone Days 112
Notes 113
References 114
About the Author 115
Beloved Aunt Vera Passes Away 116

The Big Event

On a cold, snowy day, March 25, 1926 to be exact, a six-pound, blue-eyed, red-headed bundle arrived at the Lloyd Lyle Williams home in Hawthorne, Wisconsin. Suspecting a delivery, Lloyd's other three children were sent down the hill to visit Grandpa Williams, never suspecting the joyful event taking place.

Hawthorne, still in its infancy, had no doctor, so my Grandma, Ida May Williams, filled this gap. She inherited the ability to care for the sick and injured from her mother, Manerva Gardner Barber. Ida May became Hawthorne's midwife and caretaker; as friends and neighbors called on her during any emergency.

She didn't have access to drugs at that time, so Grandma used what was available to her. Tea brewed at her home all the time, and she would make a poultice of wet tealeaves to put on burns. She also made a dressing of salt pork or bread and milk to use on infections. Kerosene, licorice, Epsom salts, tincture of iodine, and green soap made up much of her medicine chest. Being very astute, Grandma knew it was time for the birth of her new grandchild. She arrived on the scene to attend to Lloyd's wife, Ethel.

Lloyd summoned his best friend, Dr. Arthur Gordon (A. G.) Wilcox, to join the party. For most people, contacting the doctor was complicated. There were no modern conveniences as we enjoy today. There was no running water or electricity in the house, nor a telephone to make the call, but that was no problem for Mr. Williams because he was the local second trick telegrapher for the Chicago, St. Paul, Minneapolis, and Omaha Railroad in town.

He dashed down the hill to the station to place an urgent telegram to his best friend, who traveled the 15 miles from Solon

Springs. Dr. Wilcox drove his snowmobile, which at that time was a Model T Ford with a ski adapter in front instead of wheels and caterpillar treads on the rear wheels, making it a motorized sled.

Model T Ski Snowmobile

In anticipation of the birth, Grandma had well water already boiling on the old wood-burning cook stove when Dr. Wilcox arrived. Lo and behold, the expected bundle did not turn out to be Gordon Arthur, but instead the stubborn, independent, adventurous Vera Estelle Williams.

It must have been an easy delivery because Mother said, "I only missed one Lady's Aid meeting, and that was for Vera's birth." That shows how natural it was to deliver babies at home during that time.

My only brother, Lyle, was disappointed to discover that he had no brother, but another girl to add to his strife. Now, he had three sisters, Vivian, Doris, and tiny Vera.

He turned to Doris, who was very excited and thrilled to have a new baby sister, and exclaimed, "Oh my! She'll never be any good at playing baseball!"

Doris just smiled. "Who knows?"

Vivian had seen it all before and wasn't very impressed. Being the oldest, watching the family grow, she thought there were enough children in the family. Vivian exclaimed, "We've got almost as many kids as Eddie Williams!" Our Uncle Eddie had seven at that time. Vivian added, "Every time we stay overnight at Grandpa Williams' house; we get another kid."

Vera Estelle Williams - 1926

Williams Family

I was born into a family who was very active and well-respected in the Hawthorne community. They supported the Presbyterian Church, the school, and town activities. My father, Lloyd Lyle, was born to William Wallace and Ida May Williams on April 29, 1895. Father was a tremendous athlete, and loved to run, play baseball, golf, fish, hunt, and swim. He had dark black hair, light blue eyes, and grew to 5-foot 11-inches.

Father obtained his knowledge of railroading by hanging around depots; learning the Morse code and listening to the townsfolk tell stories of the good old days. Among the greatest storytellers was his father, Billy, as his friends called him. He was the local sheriff and owner of the only livery stable and saloon in town, which was right across the tracks from the depot.

Lloyd Lyle Williams - 1912

Father joined the railroad at the age of 17 on May 27th, 1912. He went wherever the railroad needed him. Since he worked a twelve-hour shift, seven days a week, he didn't get much time to relax. However, he did join the Itasca Masonic Lodge in Superior, at the same time as his good friend, Dr. Wilcox.

Father and a fellow agent on the railroad, George Schueler, also bought and operated an ice cream parlor and pool hall in town. It was a place for the men to meet and have a little recreation. Besides playing pool, they could buy tobacco, soda pop, candy, gum, and ice cream.

On July 26, 1916, Lloyd married the love of his life, Ethel Elvira Wattman. She was an attractive Swedish woman who presented herself in a stately manner. As a full-blooded Swede, she was slender and at 5-foot l0-inches, tall for a woman, had blue eyes and brown hair.

Ethel Elvira Wattman - 1914

The Wattman family was well-established in Hawthorne. Jakob August ("Gus") Wattman was one of the early pioneers in the history and development of this small town. He was born May 7, 1866, in Hudiksvall, Gävleborg, Sweden. He had red hair and blue eyes. At the age of 19, he left Sweden and sailed to the U.S., where he jumped ship and headed to Wisconsin.

It was on one sunny day in 1890, at the railroad station in Hawthorne, where he met his future wife. Gus was sitting on the baggage truck with his "cronies," watching the passenger train arrive. When the train stopped, a petite, 5-foot 2-inches, 90-pound, Swedish lady with curly black hair and baby blue eyes stepped onto the platform.

Her name was Hilda Sophia Johnson from Skona, Smöland, Sweden. Hilda was born on January 6, 1866. She had come to visit her sister, Emmeli Lindberg. Emmeli had been writing glowing accounts about Hawthorne, begging her sister to come to America to visit her. When Hilda asked for directions, Gus was only too happy to escort her to her sister's home. He scooped up her baggage and escorted her to the Lindberg's, across the tracks to a house on the side of the big hill.

When Gus came back to the depot, he told the men, "That's the woman I'm going to marry." True to his word, on November 22, 1891, Hilda Sophia Johnson and Jakob "Gus" Wattman were the first couple married in Hawthorne. Ethel was born on January 12, 1894. She was the second of eight children born to Hilda and Gus.

When my parents married, they moved into the only house on the east side of the Middle River that survived the great fire of 1910. It was set back on the hill near the millpond. The young couple lived there for about three years. When the creamery on top of the big hill on the west side of Hawthorne failed in 1918, the farmers in the area put it up for sale. Father purchased it and remodeled it into a home.

Lloyd Williams Home in Hawthorne, Wisconsin

Like most men in the community, Father loved to play baseball. He was truly a gifted athlete, even as a child. By the time he was twelve years old, he was playing on the adult team in Hawthorne. Grandma Ida May felt it was too much of a strain on her young son, so when the team came to pick him up, she insisted that he could only play five innings.

Between jobs, he played baseball in the community. For recreation, Father attended professional baseball in Superior, the Twin Cities, and Chicago, where he met Babe Ruth and other young players. At one game, Father caught a fly ball hit by the Babe, who signed it after the game. I still have that ball today.

Father thought he'd like to become a professional baseball pitcher for a major league. In 1919, he took a permanent job pitching for a team in Winnipeg, Canada. It paid $150 per month. He took a leave of absence from the railroad, where he earned only $52.50 a month and joined the team. His unique contribution to the team was as a left-handed pitcher.

Lloyd Lyle Williams – 5th From Left

However, he found that the pay was not sufficient to support his wife and young daughter, Vivian Vendela Williams. Baseball paid more, but when the players had to pay room and board as they traveled, he lost more money than he made. Plus, he missed his family back home in Hawthorne, so he gave up professional baseball and returned home to continue working twelve hours a day, seven days a week as a telegrapher.

Father's friend, George Schuler, was the depot agent at Hawthorne. He was also a talented artist and cartoonist, who drew many sketches and comic strips. To relax, he'd paint portraits. We still have an oil painting of our sister, Doris, which he created for Father, as everyone thought she was such a beautiful child.

George Schuler entered and won many area contests. I recall one that he won, naming an ice cream bar "Eskimo Pie." Here's a drawing that George drew in 1920 after Father went back to work for the railroad. It shows how money is just chicken feed to those who have it. The sketch is titled, "Lost, Strayed or Stolen."

"Here Chick, Chick, Chick!"

Mother gladly stayed in Hawthorne. Friends and neighbors knew her for her open hospitality. Every weekend, someone stopped by to sample her delicious home-baked desserts, often arriving on Saturday nights when the children were in the midst of our weekly bath. Much to our chagrin, we were all standing naked in line for the weekly plunge into the family washtub. One neighbor, in particular, regularly chose that time to come.

I remember Doris was always first in line to the washtub. It was when the water was the cleanest and must have influenced her choice in a profession, as she became a nurse later in life.

My mother was also a very talented seamstress, who made her family's clothes using all materials available, including colorful flour sacks, which she made into tablecloths, napkins, curtains, and fancy bloomers. She loved to bake, and boy did we ever have flour sacks. "Get as many flour sacks that match as you can," she'd tell Father. Then, she'd have enough material for a full dress, skirt, or blouse.

Mother could sew anything. She never bought a pattern, but she would make her own out of newspaper. Vivian would frequently come home, after window shopping for hours, and describe the latest designs. Mother would measure and draw, and then she'd hunt for the best deals on material, usually getting everything for half price. Many times she'd use old, outdated dresses or clothing. Before we knew it, a new dress in the latest fashion was hanging in the closet.

One day, Mother got a box of leather scraps from Aunt Helen. I didn't have a coat, so she sewed each of those scraps together and made me a leather jacket. She lined it with white material, and I used that jacket until it nearly fell off me.

We were the envy of the neighborhood when Mother made us Mickey Mouse sweatshirts. She got a great deal at a sale on men's underwear. She dyed them a bright orange and made us each a sweatshirt. Then she painted Mickey Mouse on the front of the shirts. I loved the first warm, soft top, but one of the problems with being the youngest child is that I got to wear Mickey Mouse for many years as I kept growing into my sister's hand-me-downs.

Mother knew that we would continue to grow during the year, so she always made everything just a little bigger than needed. Then it would still fit by the end of the year. She would make sure everything that she made had a long hem in it, so we could let it out as needed. She even bought our shoes a size too large, so we had to stuff paper into the toes. One year, I wanted boots for trout fishing. She got a pair so big, that whenever I took a step, my foot would come out of the boot. It took forever to walk in the water. I never did outgrow those boots.

I was never much for dresses. I only had two. Mother washed one, while I wore the other. I'd rather wear jeans, so when my Aunt Myrtle sent Lyle a few pairs, I was glad they were too small for him. I just rolled up the pant legs, and they fit me perfectly.

Vera Williams by Hawthorne Depot - 1930

During the summer, Mother grew fresh vegetables and fruit. We'd go berry picking in the woods, and she canned all summer long. We had canned blueberries, peas, beans, corn, pickles, fish, and chicken. She would can enough food to last us through the winter. Mother's idea of relaxing was sitting down to mend, crochet, knit, tat, or do some type of handiwork. Because of her homemaking abilities, she was able to stretch Father's meager paycheck, and none of us ever realized that we were poor.

As I grew older, I inherited Father's agility and love of sports, along with Mother's height and build. I also inherited the vehemently red hair and blue eyes from my Grandpa Wattman, on Mother's side of the family, and from Great-Grandmother Manerva Barber, on Father's side of the family. I had freckles and fair skin to accompany the red hair.

Unfortunately, I missed the gene giving me Mother's homemaking skills, including cooking, baking, and sewing. Just so you know, it wasn't for lack of trying. I stuck it out through Home Economics classes, but following my mother's frugal footsteps only got me into trouble. My teacher, Miss Wolford, instructed us on how much material we'd need to make a blouse. I went home and told my mother how much material I needed. Mother said, "Oh that's way too much. It'll go to waste!"

I went back to tell my teacher what my mother told me. Miss Wolford wasn't too sure about my skills at economizing, but she said, "If your mother thinks that's too much, then get what she thinks is best."

Home Ec. wasn't my favorite subject, and my skills at sewing were lousy, so I ran short of material when we had to cut out our blouse. I could see that I'd need some extra work, or I'd get a poor grade, so I went to class early the next morning. When I got to class, I noticed that Miss Wolford had on a new dress.

Now, my father always complimented us on our new clothes, so I repeated what he always said, "Gee Miss Wolford, you look just like a new saloon in a fog!"

Miss Wolford looked shocked and asked, "What did you say?"

Being quite naïve, I repeated it. When I realized that she didn't take it as a compliment, I could tell that my grade was slipping further. Later, in the year, I guess Miss Wolford felt sorry for me and thought she might help my appearance. She pulled me aside and asked, "Vera, could you put a little curl in your hair?"

I explained that my hair wouldn't curl. I'm sure my teacher had a hard time understanding this since my mother was a very dignified woman. She always stood tall, wore a large hat, and was prim and proper. Mother was a real lady. Surely, some of her etiquettes would rub off on me, but alas, it didn't. I tried to curl my hair. Vivian even put it in rollers, but my hair turned into a hopeless heap of frizz, worse than Orphan Annie's hairstyle.

It didn't matter to my mother how I looked, she adored me anyway. She wrote in my autograph book:

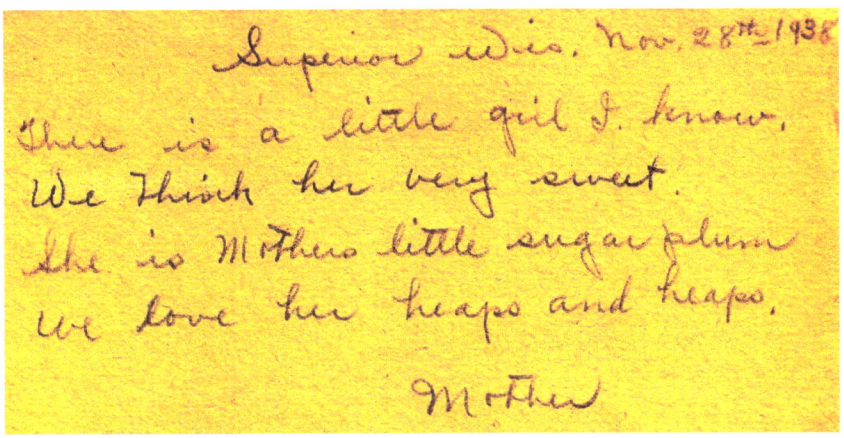

Vera's Mother's Love Was Unconditional

My father seemed to understand me quite well. He accepted the fact that I was a tomboy. Whenever he left town to attend a union meeting or a convention, he'd always bring us back a treat. Usually, he'd bring each of us a Nut Goodie. When he went to the convention in New Orleans, he returned with a special gift for each of us. He bought Vivian and Doris linen suits. Lyle got a white suit with two pairs of pants, just like Mother always told him to do. Knowing that I would never wear a dress, he bought me a pair of white pants, suit jacket, and a shirt, like Lyle's. Whenever I needed to dress up, I wore that suit everywhere. I'd ask, "Why wear a dress? It just gets in the way."

One evening, I went to the theater. I tucked my hair under a cap, and I was all dressed up in my fancy suit. During the movie, I had to go to the bathroom, so I was just entering the girl's room when the attendant stopped me saying, "You can't use that one. You need to use the boy's room." That put me in a real dilemma. I waited until everyone filed out of the boy's room, and then I went inside quickly and did my business.

Vera in Her Fancy Suit (Left) Standing By Her Sister Vivian

Now that I think about it, I never had a store-bought dress until I was 21 years old, when my stepfather, Axel gave me $20 for a new dress. He told my mother, "Vera doesn't have enough clothes to flag down a handcar!" However, it mattered little, because my favorite attire was a pair of overalls and a painter's cap. My Uncle Cecil once commented, "Vera was years ahead of her time."

The best thing that can happen to a child is to have good parents. Education was highly stressed in my family, as was hard work, honesty, and persistence. I still live by these rules.

As our parents would have it, our lives ran on railroad time. Schedules were everything. We got up when we heard the morning freight train come rumbling by our home. We had to be home by the noon train for lunch and be in bed by the evening train. It came as no surprise to Mother that I wanted to work for the railroad. It was a path less traveled by women in those days. There were only five women telegraphers in my district.

Hawthorne, Wisconsin

It's amazing how our forebears managed to find their way to Hawthorne, Wisconsin. People from France, Ireland, Norway, Sweden, and other European countries landed on the east coast, and when it became too crowded, they moved west using the waterways of the Great Lakes and rivers for transportation. Many early pioneers who came to settle in the wilderness of Northern Wisconsin and Douglas County encountered similar problems and experiences as those of our ancestors, the Williams and the Wattmans. There were no roads, no cars, and no railroads. Much of the land was still wilderness.

When the government passed the Homestead Act in 1862, it brought settlers to Douglas County. Anyone, 21 years of age or older, was granted a claim up to 160 acres of public land for $18. Many adventuresome souls traveled overland by horse and wagon on rutted trails and grassland to find a plot of undeveloped land. If the plot was "improved" by building a dwelling and cultivating the soil within five years, the settler received a title for the land.

By 1870, the richly wooded lands surrounding Hawthorne provided timber for paper mills and construction. However, there was limited transportation for the long distances between the saw mills and the markets. Plus, the bitter cold winters limited the loggers' use of the waterways, making the lumber industry a seasonal trade. Once the railroads were built, loggers could ship lumber year round.

Not only was lumbering a major occupation in Wisconsin and Minnesota, but the fertile soil grew vast amounts of wheat for the growing nation. River routes were limited, and most of the woodlands and farmlands were landlocked. To sell the wheat, farmers shipped their harvest to Superior, which was the closest market.

Farmers got more money if they shipped their grain to Minneapolis, but that was over 150 miles away. The transportation cost for wheat was $0.15/ton for every mile shipped over land. Farmers were paid only $1.10/bushel for their crop. If they were lucky, they barely broke even. Most farmers lost money.

However, the cost of shipping by rail was one-tenth that of other methods, at only $0.015/ton. At this rate, farmers made money and could ship all the way to Minneapolis, where the price was up to $1.50/bushel.

In 1881, the Northern Pacific was built in Superior. In 1884, the Omaha extended its rail line from Superior Junction (Trego) north to West Superior. This railroad was known as the Chicago, St. Paul, Minneapolis, and Omaha Railroad. In 1892, the Duluth, South Shore, and Atlantic Railroad recognized the value of the vast area of virgin timber and pristine lakes, so it extended lines from Superior across Northern Wisconsin to Michigan. The lumber industry grew steadily to form the backbone of the state's economy by the middle of the century.

Northern Pacific Steam Engine

With the coming of the railroads, the settlement of Hawthorne was in its infancy. Although some say the town was named because of the beautiful Hawthorne bushes growing there, it's more likely named for W. B. Hawthorne, the operator of the first logging camp in the vicinity. This little town was located about 25 miles south of Superior, nestling at the foot of a big hill, one of the highest points in Douglas County.

Topographically, Douglas County varies from level, swampy lowlands to gently sloping and rolling uplands. The lowest point in the county is approximately 605 feet above sea level in the City of Superior on the Lake Superior Lowland. From this point, the land rises to nearly 1,200 feet above sea level at the town of Hawthorne, towards the center of the county, and then falls to approximately 1,063 feet in the southern portion of the county.

In 1885, part of the Hawthorne Hill, west of the railroad tracks, was cut down and used to fill the Tamarack Swamp east of the railroad, where the stores, town hall, and other buildings were located. Some of the sand from this hill was taken by rail to Itasca, where it was used to fill in the banks of Bluff Creek and the Itasca Railroad yards.

In Hawthorne, the main railroad line ran east of the present line. The first depot was built of wood and was very small, only eight by ten feet. The depot agent at that time was Louis Efaw, and Joe Ackerman was the first telegrapher. The old depot burned down during the great fire of 1910.

Fortunately, the huge water tank survived the fire. It was used for the steam engines and helper engines. Steam increased the power of the freight trains coming from Superior up the steep grade to Hawthorne. The helper engines took on water and returned to Itasca to help the next train. Roll Peterson and George Schueler were two early operators of this water tank. The arm on the tank was called a Penstock. It was used to draw up the water from the nearby Middle River to put in the tank and then to put water into the steam engines to create power for the next trip.

Since Hawthorne was a very busy station, the railroad built a new depot. They kept the business operating 24 hours a day, 7 days a week. George Schueler became the new Depot Agent, and Father worked the second shift for about 23 years. William O'Shaughnessy, Ed Williby, and Jack Goodwin were three of the men who worked the third trick.

Old Hawthorne Depot – Early 1900

The main line and the passenger tracks were in front of the Depot in Hawthorne, and behind the Depot were the tracks to the stockyard and the loading tracks. There was a "Y" northeast of the Depot for the "Dobie Dinkey" to Lake Nebagamon. This track was used to haul lumber from the logging camp in Lake Nebagamon, which went through the small town of Dobie, thus giving the train its name, and the line ended in Hawthorne. The logs were then loaded onto the main freight train and shipped to Superior.

As with many small towns, the depot was the center meeting place for the community. Most of the men in town would gather there in the evenings. The fellows sat in the station or on the express cart outside listening to the jokes and tales Father told between the train orders. He loved imitating the foreign dialects as he embellished his tall tales.

*Hawthorne, Wisconsin in 1906, Depot on Right
(Where Lloyd Williams Worked)*

Hawthorne's new depot was a typical wooden structure, consisting of a loading dock and a freight storage unit. There were two waiting rooms - one for men and the other for women. Both waiting rooms had a front and rear door so that people could go out to the segregated outhouses in back. There were two waiting rooms because no respectable woman would sit with her children to wait for the train where men were swearing, smoking, and spitting tobacco juice into a spittoon. Each waiting room had a pot-belly stove, coal bucket, stove-poker, benches, a ticket window and a board showing the arrival and departure of passenger trains. The office was between the waiting rooms.

Lloyd worked at a long desk in front of a protruding bay window so that he could view the tracks from either direction. On the long desk was a switch box with a jack for three relays - one for the train dispatcher, one for general messages to run trains from station to station, and the third was the Western Union Line. Every station had its own call code. When the telegrapher heard his station's call, he plugged into the sounder. For Hawthorne, the station's call was "WN." In Morse Code, W is dot, dash, dash and N is dash, dot.

When Lloyd heard WN, WN, WN, he answered the call by opening his key, which broke the circuit, then repeated "WN." He closed the key so the dispatcher could continue his message.

Most operators placed a 'Prince Albert" tobacco can in the sounder to make the message louder.

Telegraph Key and Prince Albert Can in Sounder

Early depots powered their telegraph system using a homemade battery. These were made in large open glass jars by placing heavy copper strips in the bottom of the jars, which were then filled with blue vitriol cubes to about one inch from the top of the jar. Water occasionally had to be added, due to evaporation. The water would sometimes run over and make a real mess under the bay window desk.

Homemade Battery

These homemade batteries were long-lasting, and they provided the power to run the sound instruments.

The station had a large switchboard mounted on the sidewall for emergencies. Frequently, during stormy weather, the line would crackle and cut out. The lineman, which was a modern-day electrician, had to transfer the line to a ground wire through the switchboard so that he could repair the broken line.

Emergency Switchboard

Before copier machines, the operator had to write multiple copies of a train order. A piece of carbon paper inserted between each sheet provided the number of copies needed. Agents wrote the train orders on onionskin paper, which required a stylist. A stylist is like the point of a pen, and it could write through the several copies. Under the last copy, there was a thin layer of tin to provide a hard surface to write on.

These multiple copies communicated the dispatcher's orders. For example, an order, "Do not exceed over 15 miles per hour between mile posts 17 to 34 due to bridge repair," would need at least 3 copies. One copy was for the conductor and one for the engineer, frequently known as the C&E. The agent retained the third copy.

It is interesting to note that the conductor was in charge of the train and had the final decision on all operations. Sometimes, this led to disagreements between the conductor and the engineer, who at times felt he should be in command.

In the early days, all train orders were written on a Form "31." The train had to stop, and the train crew, including the engineer and conductor, each had to sign personally and pick up their order before the train could proceed to the next station. The reason for the signatures was to make sure that the train and engine crew understood their orders. However, frequently stopping the train caused delays.

The Northern Pacific took delays very seriously, so much so, that the railroad discontinued this form. The trains ran strictly on a time schedule. Precision was mandatory. Trains left the depot on time and had to arrive at the next station on time. If two trains had to meet, one train was pulled off on a siding to wait for the other train to pass safely. If delay occurred, the waiting train would be even further behind schedule.

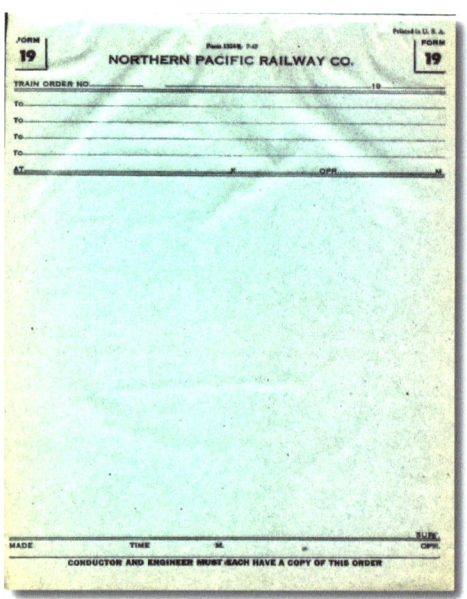

Northern Pacific - Form 19

Form 19 took the place of the Form 31. An agent handed up the train order to the engineer and conductor, using a bamboo hoop, as the train passed by, so the train did not have to stop.

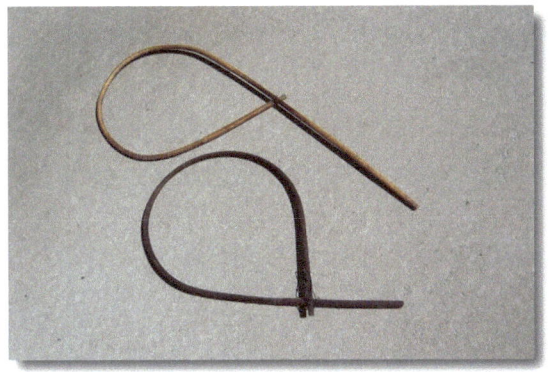

Round Bamboo Hoops

The telegraph operator's job was to deliver the order to the passing trains, giving them their instructions for each leg of their journey. The operator clipped the message to the bamboo hoop and then stood next to the railroad track, leaned forward, and held up the hoop for the engineer. As the locomotive raced by, sometimes as fast as 50 miles per hour, the engineer reached out the cab window and grabbed the hoop. After the engineer had taken the order off the hoop, he threw it beside the track, and the operator had to retrieve it.

As soon as the hoop passed to the engineer, the operator stepped away from the tracks to inspect the train for hot boxes. That means to look at the wheels to see if any were on fire. If a hot box occurs, the operator will hold their nose while pointing at the ground as the conductor passed by. This wasn't easy because the operator had to move in closer to hand the order to the conductor while also making this sign.

Handing up train orders was always dangerous because I had to stand very close to the oncoming train to pass off the orders. Sometimes logs and other debris fell from the train and injured an operator. It was dangerous, especially during winter when a snowplow protruded from the engine. Worst of all were those freezing cold, pitch black nights where I'd have to stand on slick ice and face that bright headlight of the oncoming locomotive.

The round hoops were replaced with a wood holder in the shape of a Y. Using a string about 6 feet long, I'd tie a slip-knot on each end, place one in the top notch of either end of the Y, and wrap the string's center around the V part of the Y. At the top between the two notched areas, the string allowed a "hole" in which the train order was placed, then the slip knots were tightened and looped around the slotted ends of the Y.

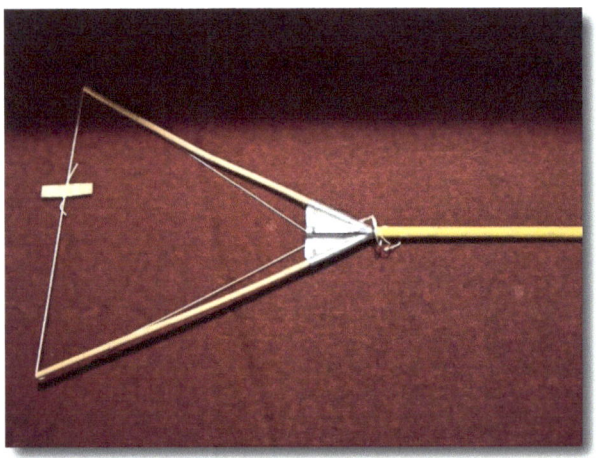

Y Bamboo Hoops

Adoption of the wire Y hoop didn't necessarily make things better for the Operator, who still had to get in close to the track to hold the hoop up for the trainman to grab.

The railroad began installing Train Order Stands sometime around the late 1940s. The agent clamped the long end of the hoop onto the stand. The trainmen then thrust their arms in the open space of the Y, pulling the string loose as they whizzed on by, getting their orders. The string was discarded. The engineer and fireman got the higher levels. The conductor on one end of the caboose and the brakemen on the other end got the lower levels.

Safety was important on the railroad, so improvements made it easier to talk to the passing trains.

The engineer knew he had an order by observing the location of the arms of the semaphore, which was located outside of the depot. Their controls were inside the depot, which consisted of two handles on a cogwheel; one going east and the other going west. The depot agent used these cogs to set the blades of the semaphore to the appropriate position for either the east-bound or the west-bound trains. Straight out at a 90° angle meant stop. A red light would come on at the top of the semaphore. When the blades were up at a 45° angle, a yellow light was displayed on top. This indicated to proceed with caution and prepare to receive the train orders. If the blades were straight up, a green light appeared on top, and it meant to proceed at full steam ahead.

Here's an example of how this works. When a train approached Hawthorne station, Father moved the semaphore in position as indicated by the dispatcher located in Superior. The dispatcher usually puts out two orders when a train is going along a single track; one to my father in Hawthorne and the other to the station in Gordon.

Dispatcher sends, "19 copy 3 east."

Father would copy back, "19 D east." This means 19 displayed east. He put the semaphore in a 45° position, and the yellow light would appear. The engineer would know to proceed with caution and receive the order."

To Gordon, the dispatcher says, "19 Copy 3 west." That meant the operator set the semaphore going west at a 45° angle. He repeats, "19 D west."

The dispatcher then notifies the station at Bennett, which is located between Hawthorne and Gordon, "19 stop east and west." The Bennett operator moves the semaphore straight out in both directions, then he repeats, "19 D stop and west." The dispatcher then addresses, "C&E stop." As mentioned before, C&E means conductor and engineer.

The dispatcher sends, "2 C&E no. 65." When the dispatcher sends a period, all three operators write the body of the message. "No. 65 Engine 2260 take siding at Bennett. Meet extra 762 engine 1520. Take siding at Bennett." The train from Gordon will see the semaphore straight across, and the engineer takes the sidetrack. He'll wait there while the train from Hawthorne goes down the line. This is so that the trains don't crash.

Now, with the advent of radio, the telegraph operator is also the radio operator. The locomotive is also equipped with a radio and as the train passes, a radio message is sent with the instructions for the train.

A series of radio and fiber optics systems have interlaced our nation, keeping trains in constant communications with a central routing system to communicate all train instructions even though it's many miles away from the speeding trains.

Before electricity, kerosene lights and lanterns lit the Hawthorne Depot. Father had to be clean and fill them with kerosene each day. He also used a small hand-held lantern as a signaling device for directing trains. These short lanterns were made of heavy steel and had a lot of protection for the globe. He swung them overhead, up and down and side to side. You can imagine the abuse these lights took.

Different color lanterns made up the signals. Red meant danger or stop. Green signaled go, and blue was for work along the side of the tracks. Yellow signals meant continue with caution, and white meant all clear. The railroad called these dead flame lanterns because they don't have an air tubule on the sides of the globe.

Here are a few lanterns that I've collected over the years.

Handheld Railroad Lanterns

The third trick operator filled the fuel buckets with wood or coal, and they had to tie train order strings, plus sweep and clean the depot. Once a week, the section crew mopped the floors. The depot agent and the early day operators had to purchase a blue serge uniform with removable brass buttons. When Father removed the buttons, the uniform served as a regular dress suit, which was the only one he owned.

Vera's Destiny

Destined to follow my father's professional footsteps, I cut my eyeteeth on a sounder and almost lost my life in front of the cowcatcher of a steam engine. This is the story of the fateful event:

The highlight of the summer season for every child in Hawthorne was the "Rainee and Sorenson" traveling tent shows. This was a series of shows brought to small towns across Wisconsin. Each night was a new movie, along with a portion of a continued serial of "The Lone Ranger."

The serial kept one wanting to go to the movie each night. During intermission, the owners sold candy and popcorn. Most of us couldn't afford such a luxury, as we had worked hard to earn the 70 cents to pay for admission to the movies (10-cent admission each night). The tent show arrived in Hawthorne in August each year.

Although this was an important event for most kids in Hawthorne, it almost proved disastrous for me. I wanted to see the serial "The Lone Ranger." However, I learned early in life that there are some things bigger than *my* wants and desires.

My parents allowed Doris and Vivian to go to the movies. They had saved their money, which they earned picking wild blueberries and selling them to Efaw's Store. Mother said I was too young to go to the movies, as the show got out late. This caused a disagreement. Being rather headstrong, I felt I was old enough to attend the movies with the other kids.

Mother tried to appease me by saying we could go down the hill and visit my friend, Ruthie Anderson. I refused to listen, and I didn't pay any attention when she told me that she was going to bring Lyle a jacket first, as it was cold, and he was playing in the schoolyard. After crying and pouting, I found I was sitting alone, so I decided to head down the hill, past the tracks to Anderson's.

My father was working his shift at the depot. A bunch of local fellows were sitting on the Express Wagon waiting for the evening train. I wasn't thinking about trains. I was just mad about not getting to see the Lone Ranger Movie.

Express Wagon or Railroad Cart

Just as I got on the tracks, someone from the express wagon called to me. I paused in the middle of the tracks to listen. Then I turned to see the "cow catcher" of the train coming straight for me.

My Uncle "Cody" (Hugh) grabbed me just before the train struck me. He had run from the express wagon when he saw what was happening. He knew the train could never come to a halt in time. He saved my life!

The engineer said he was trying to brake, but never could have stopped in time.

My mother said she was looking down from the schoolhouse hill and exclaimed, "Oh, that can't be Vera!"

Uncle Cody set me down after he saved my life, and I proceeded to walk to Andersons, realizing that my vindictive action had nearly cost me my life.

Great Depression

In 1929, when I was three years old, the stock market crashed forcing the nation into the "Great Depression." Many banks closed. If people could get their savings out of their banks, they put it under their mattress or buried it in glass jars. Many people lost their jobs. My family was fortunate because Father had a steady job, which was a rarity during the depression.

In order to save the country, President Roosevelt initiated many federal programs to provide jobs for the unemployed. These included the W.P.A. (Work Projects Administration), C.C.C. (Civilian Conservation Corp.), and the N.Y.A. (National Youth Act). Every town felt the economic effect of the depression.

Everyone in the community had to be frugal. Many survived by living off their home gardens and small farm produce. Families sent their children to the youth conservation camps to learn new skills. These included working in the forest clearing land, shoveling snow, or building public structures. The youth population moved from the big cities to the rural areas where they could get employment. Most sent part of the money they earned back home to help sustain their families.

During this time in Hawthorne, the youth built a fire tower on the highest hill in Douglas County, which was across the road from my home. They built a new elementary school in Solon Springs, and Gordon got a town hall. Youth camps were built everywhere by the C.C.C. Our Uncle, Dr. Allen A. Smith, got a job as administrator of a camp at Brule, where he taught the youth and oversaw many conservation projects.

The railroads cut back employees, just like every other industry. This meant the elimination or consolidation of many telegrapher jobs. After 23 years of steady work, Father's job as second trick operator in Hawthorne was eliminated. However, there was a job at Gordon, Wisconsin, which was only 25 miles from home. Bidding on a job was based on seniority on the Omaha Railroad. Since Father started work in 1912, he had more seniority than the telegrapher agent at Gordon, so he bumped into that position.

The road between Gordon and Hawthorne was not in very good condition, and it cost too much money to drive home every night. Therefore, Father drove to Gordon every Sunday night, slept on a cot in the depot during the week, and came back to Hawthorne after his shift on Saturday evening. Every day, my mother sent one of the children down to the depot with a fruit jar of hot food wrapped in a newspaper to keep it warm. We gave the jar to the baggage man on the evening train as it stopped in Hawthorne. He'd hand off the food to Father as they stopped in Gordon. Father bought food at the store and made a sandwich for his other meals, but once a day, my mother made sure that Father got a hot, home-cooked meal.

Lloyd Williams at Newton Tower

During the summer of 1935, our Father transferred to a more permanent job at the Newton Avenue Tower in Superior East End. We all, including "Cubby," our police dog, moved from Hawthorne to a new home in East End Superior, which was called "Old Town," because that was where the City had its first settlements.

The first City Hall was on 5th Street or Main Street, which was near the railroad tracks. Nelson Dewey was the name of the elementary school. Junior and senior high students attended East Junior/High School, respectively. This area had six churches: Episcopal, Catholic, Methodist, Presbyterian, and two Lutheran. East end was made up of several businesses. There was Euclid Hotel, a public park, St. Francis Hospital, a library, and two drug stores (East End and Poolers). There was also a dime store, bank, NP depot, post office, barbershop, bakery, doctor and dental offices. A curling and skating rink were used for recreation, plus a candy store, Lederman's Clothing Store, Merrill's Garage, a gas station, taverns, and many home-owned grocery stores (Nelsons, Smiths, Pezarks, Bullins, Schnells, Collins) rounded out the establishments. You could phone and order your groceries, and most family stores delivered the order, free of charge.

We rented a house near the park by the railroad tracks. Vivian enrolled at Superior State Teacher's College. Doris enrolled in the tenth grade at East High School. Lyle was in the seventh grade at East Junior High, and I was in the fourth grade at Nelson Dewey.

The move from rural Hawthorne to the City of Superior was monumental. Mother had over 700 jars of canned goods and all our furniture to move. Superior was also a complete change in lifestyle. Not only did we have electricity, but we also had running water, gas, and sewage, plus a telephone. We lived near the park and the railroad tracks, so Father could walk to Newton Avenue Tower to work. We only lived three months in the house near the park in East End, as this house had no insulation, and it was cold.

Then, we moved to 1631 East 5th Street, a block from East High School. This house was well insulated and owned by Mr. Warner, a carpenter. Our family had a gas stove in the kitchen and a coal-burning heater in the living room with a vent above it to heat the upstairs. It was warm, especially in the large bathroom upstairs where the hot-water tank was located. In this bathroom, Vivian had a study table, lamp, and typewriter by the window, where she studied. Doris would sit in the empty bathtub with a pillow to her back while reading Zane Grey novels."

I felt that I didn't gain much in this move, as there were only three bedrooms. I had to sleep between Doris and Vivian until Vivian graduated from college and left home. I couldn't believe that Lyle had a full bedroom to himself, although Cubby often sneaked in to share it with him.

Our dog, Cubby, also adjusted to the change. Each night he would accompany our father to the Newton Avenue Tower, protecting him from the tramps. One bitterly cold night, about 30° below zero, Father had to "spike the rail between the frog," so that the railroad tracks could be moved by a lever in the tower to switch the train to another rail line. A frog is the crossing point of two rails.

A One-Piece Cast Railroad Frog

Railroad tracks are constantly moving under the weight of the heavy locomotive and the train cars. The rails expand with heat and contract with cold temperatures. In the summer, heat kinks occurred and in the winter, they pull apart at the jointed rails. The tracks must be in perfect alignment to allow the train to go over the rails. The frog is designed to ensure the wheel crosses the gap in the rail without "dropping" into the gap; the wheel and rail profile ensures that the wheel is always supported by at least one rail.

Work to maintain the tracks was a never-ending job. Usually, a rail crew cared for the tracks, but that responsibility fell to the operator once the crew went home. Father would stand out in blizzard conditions and hack at the ice until he was able to break it apart and remove the chunks between the frog.

That night, it was so cold that Cubby froze his feet as he stood with Father. His paws became so tender that Mother made some booties to tie on his feet when it was cold. From then on, each night Cubby waited to have these booties tied on before he accompanied Father to work.

Since Father worked the night shift at the Tower, he and Cubby would meet me in the morning, when I was on my way to Nelson-Dewey School. I remember one morning when Father reached into his watch pocket and gave me a penny or two for candy. He pulled out his railroad watch to get me the money, and as he put the watch back, it slipped out of his gloved-hand, bouncing on the sidewalk. The watch broke, and since we were in the Great Depression, Father couldn't afford to get it repaired or buy another one. I still have this watch, and it's still in need of repair.

Father slept during the day because he worked at night. Mother was a perpetual house cleaner. One day while Father was sleeping, Mother decided to wash the walls and ceiling in the kitchen. The job was about complete as she stood on the kitchen table reaching for the ceiling over the sink. She accidentally slipped and fell, hitting her head on the sink.

Father heard the crash and came running down the stairs to find her on the floor. Her head was bleeding, so he took her to Dr. Wilcox, who bandaged it. When I came home for lunch, everything was ready, as usual. I was upset to see Mother had a bandage on her head, but it didn't stop her from having a hot lunch ready to eat. Mother, later in life, was diagnosed with Parkinson's disease. We believe this was a result of her fall.

Mother was a dignified woman who had definite morals, especially regarding the consumption of alcohol. However, we always had beer for company and a drink for the Coal man. Why she gave the man who delivered coal a drink, we never could comprehend. One day, our Father brought home a bottle of wine. He told Mother that she should take a drink to stimulate her appetite as Mother ate very little and was a tall slim woman. Mother refused to do this, and the wine remained in the cupboard. Finally, Father said to Mom, "You might try giving Vera a little each day to stimulate her appetite as she is so skinny." Mother agreed, and after a while, I served myself at breakfast time, but instead of the small amount like Mother gave me, I took a whole glass full.

Soon, I found it difficult to read and do math while in school. I never liked math anyway, but everything looked green and jumped around. I got so tired that I kept going to bed earlier and earlier each night. One day, Mother opened the cupboard and was horrified to see a nearly empty wine bottle. She showed my Father who exclaimed, "My God, you're sending the kid to school – drunk!" My appetite was stimulated, but no more wine for me! To my surprise, my math scores improved dramatically.

During the Depression, I had to walk everywhere I went, or else I had to take a bus. It cost 5 to 10 cents one way. However, Lyle was lucky to purchase an old 28" bicycle, which he painted bright red. He called his bike "Mr. Hawthorne." It didn't have a seat, but Mrs. Nordholm, a close friend of the family, got one from Sears, ordered by mistake. She gave it to Lyle. Oh, that didn't set very well with me. I was jealous of my brother's great fortune.

One day, I pretended to be sick and stayed home from school. I was feeling okay in the afternoon, so I took Lyle's bike, pushed it off the porch, but couldn't get on the seat. The bicycle was a boy's bike, so it had a bar across the frame. I discovered that I could pedal it if I put my feet through the frame. I was having fun when Lyle came home and caught me trying to ride his bike. He chased me until I fell and skinned my knees. Lyle didn't care that I was hurt. All he cared about was his dumb bicycle. He checked the bike to see if I had damaged it. To this day, Mr. Hawthorne is still in the family. Lyle taught his girls to ride it, and his son, Lloyd, used to "ride like the wind" on it in Alexandria, Minnesota.

Lyle & Jill Williams on Mr. Hawthorne (Lyle's Bike)

I had to wait until 1937 to get my bike. As luck would have it, I had an appendix attack when I was in the fourth grade. My father said, "If you don't need surgery, we might be able to afford a bicycle for you." Oh, how I wanted that bicycle, so I denied having any pain and gritted my teeth. On May 27, 1937, Kelly-Howe Thompson Wholesale of Duluth, Minnesota, delivered to our home at 1831 E. 8th Street in Superior, a black and orange "Schwinn World Bike" with balloon tires. I used this bike for transportation all during the Depression and during the years I worked on the Northern Pacific Railroad.

Vera on 1937 Schwinn Bicycle

Now, Lyle was jealous of my shiny new bike, and I wouldn't let him ride it. Laughing, I remember saying, "Serves you right, since you wouldn't let me ride yours." Doris and Vivian never had a bicycle and never learned to ride one. I still own this bike, and it is one of my most prized possessions. It represented freedom to go anywhere. I even rode it on a trip to Canada.

As for my appendix, that was removed when I had a major attack in 1944. Unlike any other railroad, the Northern Pacific had its own hospital for employees only, but it was located in St. Paul, Minnesota, which was too far to go during an emergency. I went to St. Joseph's Hospital in Billings Park, and the railroad paid for the operation. Health care was even affordable back then.

Working on the railroad had its advantages. Employees got an "Annual Pass" that allowed our whole family to ride the train for free. Lyle and his best friend, Gene Goodwin, who also worked on the railroad and had a free pass, decided to go West by rail. Since the boys couldn't afford to eat on the train, their mothers packed a suitcase of food for the trip.

Mom said, "Lyle, be sure to eat in a high class, clean restaurant as you travel."

The boys followed the directions given to them to the letter. They would select a restaurant, open the suitcase with their food and order a glass of milk to go with their meal.

When Lyle told about their experiences after they got home, Mother was horrified. She couldn't believe they stretched their food supply and used no money to buy food on the whole trip, except for glasses of milk.

Lyle said, "We had a good time, and it really doesn't cost much to travel first class."

My father, Lloyd Williams, served many years as a local chairman of the Order of the Railroad Telegraphers. He worked closely with Mr. Bill Liddane, who was the General Chairman of the Order. Under Mr. Liddane's leadership, the telegraphers went from a twelve-hour workday, down to eight-hour shifts, but it wasn't until I worked on the railroad on September 1, 1949, that we finally got a five-day workweek.

Lloyd Williams & Bill Liddane – 1938

My Father took over Mr. Liddane's position as General Chairman after his retirement. He arranged to do the Union job in Superior, so that Lyle and I could complete our school year, and then we planned to move to the Twin Cities in 1940.

Unfortunately, Father became ill near Christmas time and had an emergency operation. He was diagnosed incorrectly as having a gall bladder attack. Father's appendix ruptured. He lived eight days, but died when gangrene set in, and the infection could not be controlled. Although Penicillin and sulfa drugs were used in the military, they were not available yet in Superior. On December 26, 1939, our father died at the age of 44, leaving our mother to support the family.

The Masonic Order, Knight Templars, conducted the funeral in full-dress uniform, plumed hats, and swords. A huge bouquet of flowers designed with the O.R.T. Emblem (Order of Railroad Telegraphers) was among the many flowers at the Temple. At the end of the funeral, the casket was carried down the steps of the Masonic Temple, through the Royal Arch, as our family followed. It was a very impressive ceremony.

L. L. Williams Dies

One of the most regrettable duties we have to perform is to announce the death of an outstanding member; one who had served the Order with distinction for many years and was held in high esteem by all who knew him.

It is, therefore, with regret that we note the passing of Brother Lloyd L. Williams, General Chairman of the Omaha System Division No. 4, on December 26, 1939, which occurred after an operation performed in an attempt to save his life.

Brother Williams became a member on August 2, 1912, and had been continuously a member ever since that date. Early in his membership he took an active part in the affairs of the Order; was elected Local Chairman, in which office he served for many years, and was elected General Chairman in January, 1939, to succeed "Bill" Liddane, who retired on December 31, 1938.

Holder of a veteran's gold medal, showing his long membership, he was a comparatively young man when he died, and the experience gained during those years fully fitted him for the duties attaching to the office of General Chairman, he serving in that capacity with distinction for himself and credit to the Order.

His many friends in both countries were shocked to hear of his untimely death, and to his sorrowing widow and relatives we extend heartfelt sympathy in their and our loss.

Lloyd Lyle Williams Obituary – Railroad Telegrapher

Our brother, Lyle, continued in the Masonic work. Lyle got Father's Masonic Ring and his Knight Templar Sword. The work of the Masons is based on religion and the highest of morals. Our mother belonged to the Eastern Star, and Vivian, Doris, and I also joined this organization, as we all felt it was a strong tie to our father, and how he felt about living.

When our father died in 1939, our mother had to raise her children on a total income of $16 a month as a railroad pension. Mother found a job at Sasner's Emporium altering clothes. She shortened skirts, pants, and made alterations to fit the customers.

Mother found a cheaper place to rent. We moved to an apartment above Howard's Tavern and the East End Drug Store. The rent was $15 per month, but it was not a convenient place to live. We had to share the bathroom with the Krenz Family. Gus Krenz was section foreman on the railroad. We had to carry our slop water from the sink to the bathroom to flush it down the toilet.

We also had to walk up 27 steps to get to the apartment. I carried my bike up those steps every day, until the policeman in East End felt sorry for the "skinny redhead" and told me I could use part of his garage. Our unit had only one bedroom, so Lyle slept on a cot in the living room. Vivian taught school in Iron River. She came home only on the weekends, and Doris was in nurses' training in St. Paul.

When we first moved to this apartment, it was a battle with the cockroaches, which we continually fought. Mother had our friend, Mr. Peterson, sand the floors, and she varnished them. Then she put up lace curtains, making it a more comfortable place to live. She enjoyed her neighbors, as they met for coffee and exchanged recipes.

Sixteen dollars a month plus the small amount of extra money she earned wasn't enough to support our family. Wold's East End Tailors and Drycleaners offered Mother a job, paying more money than Sasner's, and she could walk a half a block to work. This job was more convenient and profitable for her.

Lyle graduated from East High School in 1941 and went to work at the East End King Midas Flour Mill to supplement the family income. He studied telegraphy at night. I became interested and bought my first key and sounder set, along with an instruction book, from Sears for $4.50. This money I earned from selling my mother's homemade bread to Axel Nordholm.

Lyle and I would practice in our living room. He rigged up the set in two rooms. Lyle was in one room, and I was in the other. We made a contest out of who could send and receive a message the fastest. Being competitive, he'd send the messages too fast for me to interpret. I would shout, "Slow up." That made him send all the faster. It was obvious I had to go to school.

In the summer of 1943, I attended Superior Vocational School using funding from the National Youth Act, a program designed to pay youth for preparing for a job. I got paid 25 cents per hour to study telegraphy.

There are in fact three forms of Morse Code. The original is called the **Continental Morse Code or Gerke Code** used throughout Europe.

The one used by railroad telegraphers is the **American Morse Code**, which revised letters c, f, j, l, o, p, q, r, x, y, and z, plus all of the numbers are different. The reason telegraphers used American Morse is because they can send it across the wire 5% faster than the other codes. American Morse is now nearly extinct—it is used most frequently in American railroad museums and in Civil War re-enactments.

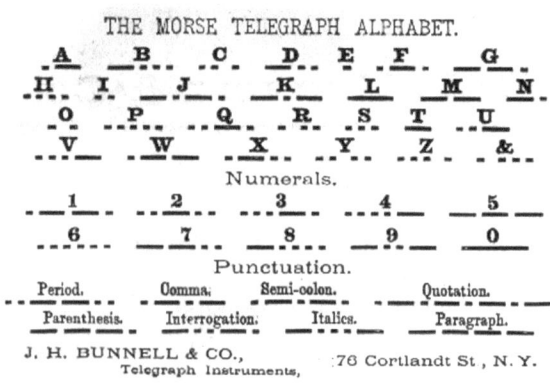

American (Telegrapher's) Morse Code

The railroad was very strict when it came to telegraphy. Each student was only allowed to take the exam three times. If he or she failed, they were unable to become a telegrapher.

"Morse Code" today virtually always means the International Morse, which supplanted American Morse. It's important not to mix the three codes. When searching for Morse Code on-line, most are International, so don't be fooled. Below is a diagram comparing both codes, so that you can see the difference.

Letter	International Code	American Morse	Letter	International Code	American Morse	Digit	International Code	American Morse
A (info)	·—		N (info)	—·		0 (info)	—————	—[1]
B (info)	—···		O (info)	———	· ·[2]	1 (info)	·————	·——·
C (info)	—·—·	·· ·[2]	P (info)	·——·	·····	2 (info)	··———	··—··
D (info)	—··		Q (info)	——·—	··—·	3 (info)	···——	···—·
E (info)	·		R (info)	·—·	· ··[2]	4 (info)	····—	
F (info)	··—·	·—·	S (info)	···		5 (info)	·····	———
G (info)	——·		T (info)	—		6 (info)	—····	······
H (info)	····		U (info)	··—		7 (info)	——···	——··
I (info)	··		V (info)	···—		8 (info)	———··	—····
J (info)	·———	—·—·	W (info)	·——		9 (info)	————·	—··—
K (info)	—·—		X (info)	—··—	·—··			
L (info)	·—··	——[3]	Y (info)	—·——	·· ··[2]			
M (info)	——		Z (info)	——··	··· ·[2]			

International vs American (Telegrapher's) Morse Code

Even though I was only 16 years old at the time, I continued the telegraphy program while finishing my Senior year of high school. It wasn't easy getting up early to take the bus to vocational school at seven in the morning. The instructor spent one hour sending Morse code to me individually. Then I hopped on the bus and quickly returned to high school to attend my scheduled classes. It cost me five cents each way.

Lyle, meanwhile, passed the Morse Code Test, and the Soo Line hired him to work the night shift at Central Avenue in South Superior. When he got paid, he gave the entire check to Mother, only keeping enough for food as he got shifted from job to job.

Gene Goodwin, Lyle's friend, went to work on the Soo Line just a few days before Lyle, so he had more seniority. Often Gene held a job just before Lyle. Gene slept and ate at the depot, and he was a messy guy. When Gene left to work at another station, he'd leave his mess behind. When Lyle came to work, he'd either have to clean up after Gene or get a reprimand from the superintendent for a dirty depot. Gene was called a "Boomer," meaning he went from railroad to railroad.

The railroad really needed all of their employees, since many were drafted to serve in World War II. All the boys at high school were getting ready for the military. We had a mid-year ceremony, so all the boys could wear their graduation regalia and graduate before the end of the school year as many left as soon as they passed their physical exams.

On April 29th, 1944, my father's birthday, I went to the Union Depot in Duluth Minnesota and passed my telegrapher's exam. I was tested on the Book of Rules required by all railroad employees and the Morse code, which only the telegrapher's had to pass. I got my certificate on May 3, 1944.

Vera's Telegrapher's Certificate From Northern Pacific

I had to read and record twenty-three words per minute. Each word had an average of five letters to a word without breaking, to pass the exam, but the vocational school required twenty-five words per minute, so I knew that I'd pass.

Timing is important when sending a message. Three dots equals one dash. The space between each letter is three dots, and the space between each word is seven dots. Each student was only allowed to take the exam three times. If he or she failed, they were unable to become a telegrapher.

Not only did we have to interpret the code accurately, but we also had to write legibly. There could be no blemishes on the train order. Many of the old-time operators could read and record at a speed of sixty to seventy words per minute. They were called a "Lightning Slinger." Some even took it on the mill, meaning they typed the message on a typewriter as it was sent across the wire. Our stepfather, Axel Nordholm, always took his messages on the mill.

Axel Nordholm at His Railroad Desk

Axel learned to decipher the Morse Code by ear, and his fingers flew across the old typewriter keys with the letters worn off from heavy use.

Lyle never attended vocational school, but he learned directly from the Soo Line dispatchers. I remember saying to Lyle one day when he was gloating over his speedy transmissions, "Well, what would you expect? You played all night, and I only get one hour every morning."

Lyle continued to work for the Soo Line in Minnesota and Wisconsin for 44 years. In Minnesota, he became an agent operator in Palisade (1948 – 1954), Clearbrook (1954 - 1961), Oklee (1961 – 1968), and then in Alexandria (1968 – 1971).

Lyle C. Williams at His Long Desk in Oklee, MN - 1963

Then as the Soo Line cut back, he was a traveling agent at many stations along the line between Glenwood, Minnesota and Frederic, Wisconsin. He retired from the railroad on February 28, 1986. Lyle lived in Alexandria, Minnesota with his wife, Rosemary, until his death on September 26, 2006.

During the hardships of the Great Depression, Mother married Axel Nordholm on July 6, 1946. His wife had died around the same time as our father. Since both were alone, it made sense to combine households. Once Mother moved in with Axel, I had a room of my own for the first time in my life. Axel always treated me well. He encouraged me to follow my dreams, no matter where they would take me.

Vera, Axel Nordholm, & Mother - 1946

My path led me to work on the extra board for the Northern Pacific Railroad for nearly 10 years, while I pursued a second career in teaching physical education for 38 years. During those 10 years, I worked at 20 different stations, mostly in Minnesota. The following chapters are the highlights of my experience.

West Duluth, Minnesota

Station name: West Duluth
Division: Lake Superior, Duluth and Superior terminals, first subdivision
Station #: L04
Telegrapher's call: WU

Upon employment on the Northern Pacific Railroad, every telegrapher and agent received two things, a rulebook and a switch key. Because the railroad used a wide variety of locks to secure switches, signals, buildings, and other facilities, employees had to have a master key that would open every lock along the line. The switch key was carefully guarded, and I carried it at all times on the job.

Switch Lock & Keys

Losing a key was once considered grounds for instant dismissal. Many a wife would safely guard the keys while her husband went out to the local watering hole, lest he lost them. Today, keys from long-gone railroads are a prized possession among collectors. They are usually made of brass, and the majority of railroad keys are a standard size, made to fit a switch lock customized for each railroad. Typically, keys were marked with a railroad's name or initials.

At the ripe old age of 18, I started my first day of work at West Duluth, Minnesota. There wasn't very much business on a Sunday, so it was considered an easy job. No one was at the depot to greet me, so I opened the door with my switch key. At that time, telegraphers were also the Ticket Agents in every town. We were also the railroad's public relations department and had to handle everything that came our way. Not knowing exactly what to expect, I sold tickets, copied train orders and messages, made the yard check, filled out the billing, and managed the cash while on duty. Fortunately, I managed to survive the day, even though I had no orientation to the job.

This isn't the only time I worked at West Duluth. I had the opportunity to work there one cold, blustery day later that winter. My stepfather, Axel Nordholm, lent me his car so that I could drive to work. As the temperature kept dipping lower, I'd run outside to start the car periodically throughout my trick, so the motor would start when I was ready to go home. There wasn't a garage or a head bolt heater in those days.

That morning, one of my customers arrived to pick up an express package at the depot. It was a basket of fruit sent from Florida. To my chagrin, the basket was a little light. On the railroad, when an order is incomplete, it's called as "bad order" and could be refused by the customer. The shipper must pay the price because the order did not meet the customer's specifications. Upon further investigation, I discovered that fruit proved to be a good dessert for the operators on those cold winter nights.

It wasn't unusual to have a bad order on the railroad. It never failed to be a "bad order" when liquor was the express package. I can't recall any shipments of liquor where at least one bottle wasn't reported broken during the shipment.

One day, while I was on duty, a conductor's wife came to the depot with a bag of lunch. Her husband had forgotten to take it to work with him. That meant I had to tie the lunch bag to the order and pass it up on the hoop. The engineer on the freight train had already received his order, so I struggled to tie the lunch, along with the train order, to the Y or fork-type hoop, and I handed it up to the conductor at the end of the train. Fortunately, the hoop had a removable string that pulled out of the hoop with little effort, when the conductor put his arm through it. It saved many a sore arm in the process. It was hard enough to grab the order, let alone a whole lunch besides. I had to get really close to the train. Luckily, one fellow didn't go hungry that night.

Central Avenue, Superior, WI

Station name: Superior - Central Avenue
Division: Lake Superior, Duluth and Superior terminals, second subdivision
Station #: 67
Telegrapher's call: AJ

I worked the "extra board" which meant that I traveled from job-to-job, 20 in total, throughout my career. Wherever the railroad had a need for a telegrapher, I was assigned to the post. I worked the Lake Superior Division on the Northern Pacific Railroad, including all stations between Duluth and Staples, Duluth and St. Paul and Duluth and Ashland, Wisconsin.

Before I finished high school, I was assigned my first job away from home. It was a real experience since I'd never stayed up all night until that time. Operators were in great demand because the service drafted many employees to fight in World War II. Special permission from the superintendent was granted for me to leave school early to report for third trick at Deerwood, Minnesota.

It was here that I received my first formal orientation on how to do my job. Mr. Henry gave me my directions. He worked the second trick, and I was working the third. He said, "I'll break you in." He stood towards the railroad tracks and pointed saying, "East is east. West is west." Waving both hands back and forth, he added, "Never the twain shall meet."

Then he showed me where to spot (park) the express wagon for the bread delivery at 4 a.m. Upon which he said, "So long. I leave you to your immediate sorrow. See you tomorrow."

That ended my formalized training, making me capable of handling all situations from there on out. Oh, what a long night that turned out to be.

The waiting room door slammed as two men walked into the depot around 2 a.m. and exclaimed heatedly, "Where are my train orders?"

I could see they weren't real happy with me, so I replied, "Where is the train?"

They pointed to the opposite wall of the depot.

It seems my formalized training was lacking. No one had informed me of the track behind the depot. The track went to Ironton, to the iron ore mines and, of course, that train crew needed orders. Once I figured that out, I thought I'd squeaked by without too much of a hassle.

But my training didn't stop there. I still had to move the express wagon to the platform to receive the bread load from the Duluth to Minneapolis passenger train. I pulled and pulled on that wagon until I nearly broke my back. Finally, I discovered there was a chain looped around the last wheel keeping the cart in place. With much effort, I moved the cart in place just in time for the 4 a.m. bread delivery. I jumped up on the express cart and started to unload. To my surprise, we unloaded for nearly 20 minutes. How one town could eat so much bread, I'll never know!

Just as I thought my unloading day was done, I was told, "Get another cart for the mail." After everything was finally unloaded, I had to pull the wagons back into the warehouse for pickup.

Whew, surely I'd done my night's worth of work. Wrong again! I entered the depot only to hear my station call, "DO, DO, DO."

I quickly broke the circuit and returned the call, "DO."

The dispatcher informed me that it was time for the section crew line up to give to the section foreman. This was done each morning, giving him his orders for the day. The train arrivals and departures are listed, so the section crew could work safely along the line and get off the tracks before a train comes down the line.

To my chagrin, this dispatcher loved having new telegraphers. To confuse the new operator, he would dispatch his messages as fast as he could send. When I couldn't follow the message, I had to break the circuit and ask him to repeat the last word. The more times I would break, the faster the dispatcher would send.

As the dispatcher listed each station, I thought the names seemed to be very strange. I'd never heard of these names before. I recall breaking on the word "Aitkin" about three times. He kept sending. Finally, I picked up the timetable and followed the stations listed. To this day, I can still spell "Aitkin". AITKIN. It will be with me for life.

I also found out that you do not make mistakes on the railroad. It's always someone else who made the mistake. Knowing that I'm somewhat honest and have somewhat good morals, as a new operator, I realized that I missed a train order. I had to put the order into a hoop and hold it up when the train went by. The bright light of the train blinded me, and I hoped the engineer would put his arm through the hoop and get the order. It wasn't easy standing there in that bright light, and I had the urge to go in the other direction. It's also hard to judge where the hoop is supposed to be, but I lifted the hoop out at a 45° angle, so the engineer could catch the string as he leaned out of the cab, while going 50 miles per hour.

Well, for some reason, the engineer missed my hoop, and he had to stop the train to get the message. So I immediately took off running after the train to get to the engine. It must have taken me nearly ten minutes before I reached the engine, handed up the order and then ran back to the caboose with the copy.

The next morning, I reported to Mr. Henry. "At 6:53 a.m., I missed the train order. I did not judge correctly where I was to stand as the train came rushing by. It was difficult to judge where to stand because of the glare of the headlight from the locomotive, and the engineer missed the hoop I handed up to him.

He said, "No, that's not what happened. You missed the order because there was a cinder in your eye."

Naively, I shook my head. "No, I didn't have a cinder in my eye. I missed the order."

Henry explained, "It was the engineer's fault. He didn't judge the order right, and you had a cinder in your eye."

Ah ha, I finally caught on. Thereafter, it appeared that on such occasions, I definitely had cinders in my eyes, but at least there was a good reason for a delay. Now that I think about it, I should be blind by now.

Quickly, I learned lesson number one…Commonly known as "passing the buck." I found out the engineer always blamed the operator, and the operator always blamed the engineer when an order was missed.

Ironton, Minnesota

Station name: Ironton
Division: Lake Superior, Cuyuna northern branch, eighth subdivision
Station #: LK4
Telegrapher's call: RN

The chief dispatcher sent me to Ironton, where the main industry is iron ore. I had been to Ironton before, and I didn't want to go because of the water supply. I told him, "It seems that when I drank the water, I could spit steel through my teeth."

However, that wasn't a good enough reason for the dispatcher. He said, "If you go to Ironton, I'll send water to you from the trains coming up from Duluth."

Having no other excuse, "Ironton, here I come!"

The job in Ironton consisted of making up the ore trains. The trainmaster and I made up the freight train's consist. It's a listing of all the types of train cars and their numbers that went to the Superior East End ore docks. The train master told me which track I was supposed to direct the engineer for placement of the ore cars.

There were three ore docks; the Northern Pacific in East-End, the Great Northern in Itasca, and the Duluth, Missabe, and Iron Range Railroad Company (DMIR) in Proctor. All of these served different mines in Minnesota. In Ironton, we worked the Cuyuna Range and shipped the ore to Superior to be loaded on the ships in the Great Lakes. That's where my Uncle Peter Rich worked. From there, the ore was placed into various pockets in the ship and delivered to the steel mills in the east.

My job was to signal the switch engine as it was coming up delivering the cars from the mine. The engine was to either "head in" or to "back in" on a given track. We used hand signals to indicate the track. I tapped the top of my head to indicate "head in" and then held out my arms indicating which track. One for track one, both arms for track two, and I pumped my arms up and down for track three. The engineer always understood that sign, but when it came to "back end," he just wouldn't comprehend.

The "back end" signal was to slap my backside and then indicate the track. The engineer tooted, meaning he didn't get the signal. So, I slapped my butt again and gave him the track signal. That's when the fun and games began. After being tooted at several times, I wised up and changed my "back in" signal to slapping the back of my hand instead of my butt, which the engineer seemed to catch the first time. Then, I put the way bills in order according to the train cars and handed it to the conductor for his consist.

There was another reason that I didn't care for Ironton. Usually, I got along with the agents quite well, but in this case, there was parting of the ways. It was the end of the week. The agent left a message on the desk stating, "On Saturday, V. E. Williams will work three hours and fifty-nine minutes."

Saturday was my only day off for the week, and I knew that four hours constitutes overtime pay. I told the agent, "I'll work four hours or eight hours, but I will not work three hours and fifty-nine minutes!"

That created considerable discussion, but finally, the agent decided he could not sway my decision, so he worked the shift himself. Working for the railroad was hard work. Like I said earlier, we did not get a five-day work week until September 1, 1949.

Taking that Saturday off, I left the Spina Hotel, where I was staying, caught the freight train to Deerwood, and I rode in the caboose. Then, I hopped on the passenger train to Duluth. When I got back to Ironton, I found out that the hotel had rented my room out while my belongings were still in it. The hotel had violated the law. They had rented out one room twice during the same timeframe, but no one seemed to think that was an offense. After that, I learned to be more cautious with my accommodations.

For recreation, I would ride on the fireman's seat in the engine, as the train was going out to the mine. The engineer dropped me off at one of the lakes, and I'd fish until the train returned. Then, I got back on the train and rode it into town.

I have always loved trains. Whenever I travel anywhere even to this day, I manage to look over the train, ride with the engineer and enjoy a relaxing journey through the countryside.

Vera on Engine #3

One day, I hitch-hiked to Brainerd with the hotel waitress. We got a ride fairly quickly. Someone who she knew picked us up. We shopped, walked around town, and then I realized it was getting late. I was getting worried about how I was going to get to work on time. I knew the depot agent wouldn't be very happy if I was late for my shift. Fortunately, I made it to work on time when we caught a ride back with someone from the town. My mother would be pleased to know that was the only time I ever hitch-hiked.

Gambling was prevalent in Ironton. It was overwhelming how pitiful it was to see poor families putting all of their income into slot machines. Gambling seemed to be everywhere in this city. Children were barefoot and in need of clothes, but their parents just kept feeding the slots. I was glad to see that soon thereafter; Minnesota removed all slot machines from the restaurants, hotels, and bars.

Motley, Minnesota

Station name: Motley
Division: Lake Superior, second subdivision
Station #: 199
Telegrapher's call: MO

When I arrived in Motley, as in other cities, I had to find lodging. Frequently, the agent would suggest a place to stay. The agent at Motley suggested that I stay at his place for 50 cents a night. I took him up on his offer because I didn't know any better.

There was only one restaurant in this town, and it was closed on Tuesdays. The agent kindly invited me to join him and his wife for dinner. After a fine meal, he suggested that I pay for one-third of the can of chili we had for supper. Looking forward to every Tuesday, I always paid my share for the meal. However, one time I must have short-changed him because as I was leaving on the train to go home for the weekend, the agent quickly boarded and demanded ten cents more. I guess I must have eaten an extra portion of chili that night.

I was becoming concerned about my accommodations. Then, I found out that this agent was one step below frugal when I heard from his wife that he even wore his dead mother's bloomers, instead of buying new underwear. I know it was during the war, but that was more information than I wanted to digest at the time.

Speaking of digestion, I realized that I might be paying more than my fair share. I decided to go to the store to buy my own food and eat it at the depot. Soon, my food was missing. I wondered if I had another rat in my office. I couldn't find a rodent, but I did find a rat. The agent was taking my food home with him and stashing it in his refrigerator. Upon my discovery, I reclaimed my possessions and moved to a new location.

I moved in with an elderly woman, Mrs. Johnson, who was simply delightful, with the same values as I had. It was the middle of World War II, and the government found it necessary to ration food, gas, coffee, tires, shoes, and even clothing during that time. I couldn't just walk into a store and buy as much sugar, butter or meat as I wanted. All these things were rationed.

Rationing started on a voluntary basis back in the early 1940s, but the plan was unsuccessful. As sugar, coffee, gasoline, and other imported supplies became more scarce; the government created a system to make sure everyone got their fair share.

In May 1942, the US Office of Price Administration froze the prices of all everyday goods. Each member of the family was awarded a ration book and stamps based on the number of people in that family. Everyone pooled their stamps together to plan their family meals. This became a real challenge. Each stamp had a number on it designating the points it was worth as well as a letter showing in which "rationing period" the stamp could be used. Point management was critical to effective shopping since the number of points available was limited by the rationing period.

We were fortunate in our family because my sister Doris was a city health nurse until she enlisted in the Army. She got B ration cards, which allowed her to get more gas than the average citizen.

At the grocery store, each rationed product had a point value assigned to it that was independent of the price. The point value fluctuated depending on how limited the item was. For instance, sugar was harder to export from Hawaii after the war started, so the points just continued to go up, the longer the war went on.

The grocers posted the current official point lists. When I went into the store, I'd have to review my list at great length to be sure I had enough stamps to buy everything that I wanted. At the checkout counter, I would remove the proper amount of stamps in the presence of the clerk. Since the grocers could not make change, shoppers were advised to use high-point stamps first.

Later, as the war continued, blue and red tokens, about the size of a dime, were issued every month, and they were worth 1 point each. Every person started with 48 blue points and 64 red points a month. New ration stamps were issued as the old ones expired.

I went to the store to buy my food to see what I could buy for the week. I could only buy based on my ration coupons, which meant I was only allowed to buy a small amount, even if I could afford more.

Meat was especially scarce during the war, and in this small town, the feed store had live chickens for sale at 50 cents each. I didn't need a ration card to get these chickens because they hadn't been processed yet. So, I came up with a great idea. I thought I could buy some chickens for my mother to can. I bought five big chickens.

This is where I encountered my first problem. How to get the chickens home? I'd ridden my bicycle to the store, so the clerk tied the chicken's feet and put them into a gunnysack. I picked up the sack, and away I went packing them on my bicycle. I was glad I had a basket in front of the handlebars. When I got to my residence, I realized that I had another problem. How to kill the chickens?

As I pondered my dilemma, Mrs. Johnson came to my rescue. Being a veteran, she said, "I'll kill them, and you pluck 'em."

Reaching into the gunnysack, she pulled out a chicken and swung it by the head until it snapped off the body. The chicken flapped its wings, and the feet broke loose of its binding as it fluttered to the ground. It stumbled all over the yard with blood spurting in all directions until the chicken was finally dead. Then she grabbed the next one.

When the chicken finally died, I grabbed the feet and dunked it into a tub of hot water so that the feathers could be easily plucked from the body. I plucked feathers, big feathers, little feathers, pin feathers. Boy, did I pluck feathers. Mrs. Johnson felt sorry for me, so she helped me dunk and pluck until they were completely cleaned. Being the expert, she could pluck twice as fast as I could. Now I had to cut and gut them and put them into the refrigerator until I was ready to go home.

Heading home for the weekend, I gathered up my chilled chicken parts and stuffed them into a box, hoping to get them home before they spoiled. My mother immediately canned them to prevent contamination. After this procedure, I'm not too fond of chicken. I'm awfully glad I didn't buy a moose. However, I did work at Moose Lake while working the railroad.

Later that year, while I was working at Motley, the conductor on the passenger train had reported that the signal light was out on the semaphore, which is a high tower at the depot. The trains have to see the signals, so they know whether or not it is safe to proceed along the track. The dispatcher called, "MO, MO, MO."

I returned the call, "MO."

The dispatcher sent, "The order board light is out. You need to fix the signal."

I have to admit, I hate heights, but I fully intended on fixing the signal light. So, I grabbed a set of pliers and any equipment I thought I'd need along with a light bulb and took the ladder to the semaphore. I placed the ladder against the tower, and up I went heading to the top of the semaphore. I'd get so far up, and the ladder would begin shaking, and down I'd come. Getting my nerve back, I tried again to go up the ladder, but again, I couldn't make it to the top. Taking a deep breath, I tried one more time, and finally, I had to admit failure.

I went back into the office, called the dispatcher and reported, "I can't fix the light. Three times I went up and three times I came down, and I just can't get to the top to change that light bulb."

The dispatcher signaled back, "Don't worry about it. Just leave a note for the agent, and he'll fix it in the morning."

When I told the agent the next morning, he wasn't very happy with me, but he changed the order board light on the semaphore.

Whenever that dispatcher was on duty, he always said, "Vera, the order board light is out, you'll need to fix the signal."

I'd run out to check the light, and it would still be on, so he just tried to get my goat. After a while, I'd just tell him, "I guess it'll have to stay out then." That made him quit hounding me.

The agent had multiple tasks to perform in the community and fulfilled many strange requests. One afternoon, a farmer drove up to the depot and asked me for a glass of water for his wife. He exclaimed, "She was dragged by a horse and is in need of help!"

I found his wife in the back seat of his car. She was all covered with dirt and not breathing. Using my first aid skills that I'd learned in school, I was unable to find a pulse. I returned to the depot to call Staples, which was the closest town with an ambulance. When the ambulance arrived, I was surprised to see it was a hearse. In many cities, they served both purposes. In this case, it was the right vehicle for the job. It was strange that this farmer remarried within two weeks.

Staples was the next station and the last one going west on the Duluth to Lake Superior route. We called it the terminal. I didn't receive many train orders at Motley because most trains were coming into the terminal. However, one night the dispatcher put out an order for an extra, which was to be a very long defense train. Unfortunately, the engineer at the head end missed the order as the train barreled through town. This meant the train had to stop. It took a mile or two before the train could halt all these cars. To avoid further delay, I dashed all the way to the head of the train to deliver the order. The train was so heavy that he had to make several attempts to start moving again. It was especially difficult because there was a slight curve to the tracks causing the conductor in the caboose to be tossed violently about. As he finally reached my hoop when the caboose passed by, he plucked off the order and blessed me. I think he used every foul letter in his vocabulary. I got the distinct impression that he wasn't very happy with me!

In Staples, the conductor had to report the delay to the operator to send on to the dispatcher in Duluth. The conductor's message read, "Delayed Motley 30 minutes account operator missed train order." However, the Staple's operator passed on a slightly modified message to the dispatcher saying, "Defense Extra delayed in Motley account engineer missed order." On occasion, there was a bit of rivalry between locomotive and operative divisions. This time the operators covered each other.

Working second trick at Motley had its disadvantages. Luckily, I was very fast on my feet in those days, as I was approached by a supervisor of the track crew. We always kept the waiting room open, no matter what hour of the day, so I made sure that the door between the waiting room and my office remained locked. I knew the track supervisor was out in the waiting room and was slightly drunk, so I put my headphones on and pretended to be talking to the dispatcher, trying to avoid him. But that didn't deter his actions. He crawled through the open ticket window and jumped into the office.

Now, I was locked inside my office with this man. I wondered, "How do I get rid of him?" Suddenly, it occurred to me that the local liquor stores in Minnesota are all owned by the city, and they closed at 11 p.m. I recall saying, "I'm really busy now, so why don't you go to the liquor store before it closes and get your last drink?" He opened the office door and left. I relocked the door and immediately slammed down the ticket window.

When my shift was over, I waited and watched. Having no relief agent working the third shift, I was alone at the depot. I knew I had to get back to my room to pick up my suitcase and return to the station to catch the train at 3 a.m. Normally, I would go through the waiting room, turn to the right to get to the main road, and go straight to my residence. However tonight, I changed the route. Finally making my move, I dashed out the office door and went through the waiting room. I bolted straight ahead instead of turning left and jumped over the park railing, running as fast as I could. At the town pump, I stopped and looked back. There was my drunken adversary waiting for me at the depot door. I was a track star that night!

There was only one liquor store allowed in each small town, and it was owned by the city. It's interesting to note that the profits from that liquor store paid for all the sidewalks and city improvements. My drunken friend was a constant contributor to this fund.

Moose Lake, Minnesota

Station name: Moose Lake
Division: Lake Superior, third subdivision
Station #: L43
Telegrapher's call: MU

Moose Lake NP Depot

At Moose Lake, I unloaded my suitcase and my trusty Schwinn bicycle, which was my main mode of transportation. I was fortunate to stay with Senator Hubert Humphrey's aunt, who was a wonderful woman. I got to meet many different people along my many travels.

One Sunday when I came to work, there was a note saying, "Vera, put on two cases of blueberries and one CORPS." Oh, I thought blueberries and something from a corporation. Okay, so I didn't proceed to pull out the wagon and spot it for unloading until I saw the train coming. When I opened the warehouse door, I found two cases of blueberries and a rough box with a corpse. Well, I noticed my mistake too late.

Whenever there's a rough box to be loaded, the agent is supposed to notify the dispatcher beforehand, so the station before would clear the opening of the baggage car ahead of time. Well, I hadn't done that, and I knew I'd made a mistake. I thought I'd be helpful, so I jumped up on the cart and had to unload some bread and then handed up the two cases of blueberries. I said, "I'll help load the box into the train. You pull, and I'll push."

So I got behind the coffin and gave a big boost, but all I managed to do was to slide over the rough box, and I landed in the baggage car next to the blueberries. I looked rather stupid in the car, and the baggage man got a big laugh out of it. The rough box was still on the baggage cart. We finally managed to get the box loaded, but I was more careful after that.

Another time, it was New Year's Eve in Moose Lake, and the temperature was 50° below zero. I knew that the temperature was right because Cedrick Adams in Minneapolis reported on the news that the coldest spot in the nation was Moose Lake at 50° below zero. I was trying to keep warm in the depot. First, I'd stand in front of the stove and warm up my front, and then I'd turn around and warm up my backside.

When the train came in, we had some jolly old engineers who were imbibing already before they met their final destination in Duluth. They were violating Rule G, rather severely. I found baggage strewn all along the platform, and I had to pick it up in that bitterly cold weather.

Wrenshall, Minnesota

Station name: Superior - Wrenshall
Division: Lake Superior, Duluth and Superior terminals, second subdivision
Station #: 82
Telegrapher's call: WQ

Talking about cold weather, later that winter, I was in Wrenshall, MN. I borrowed my step-father's car. It was a Chevrolet, and I got lost a few times, but I finally found the station. It wasn't easy because the last operator had burned down the depot, and now the office was in a boxcar. When I got there, I opened the door with my switch key. Well, there wasn't much to keep the wind out, and it was so frigid, I could see my breath while trying to work.

The telegraph wire was repeating, "WQ, WQ," which is the code name for the station. My fingers were so cold I could hardly write the message, and my feet were freezing. I looked around me and found an empty coal bucket near the stove, so I looked for some coal. There wasn't any. Then I looked for kindling and some wood. Still nothing. I opened the door, and there wasn't even a tree in sight. The only thing I could find to burn was an old empty coal shed. I tore off the door, took it into the station, and carved some kindling, and then I burned that door. By 4 a.m., it got so warm that I was afraid to leave the building for fear that the boxcar would burn to the ground just like the depot had done, so I stayed an extra hour to work until the fire died down.

My ordeal inspired a little poem I wrote at that time, and Jill found in my files:

Agent Wrenshall was the call.
There dashed Williams on the ball.
Train orders, messages, and freight to haul,
But that didn't bother her at all.

The best was the old stove fire,
Where dirt and soot had little to aspire.
The town was little and hard to find,
But Axel's car kept it on the mind.

It's all over tomorrow, hip, hip, hurray!
For I couldn't stand it another day.

That about sums up my stay at Wrenshall.

Carlton, Minnesota

Station name: Carlton
Division: Lake Superior, Duluth and Superior terminals, second subdivision
Station #: 86
Telegrapher's call: UN

    I also worked at Carlton, MN, which was a very busy station. There were two telegraph desks. Sitting down in a swivel chair, I'd take an order from one dispatcher in the third district, and then turn around and take another order from the second district. At first, I wasn't sure I ever wanted to work at this station, but Mr. Wigg, the Chief Dispatcher, thought I could handle the job, so I found myself on duty.

    He even said, "If you work on Christmas, I'll put an extra man on to help with unloading." That was unusual since a woman agent never got anything extra. I wrote a poem about this town too.

> The red headed teacher homeward bound,
> To spend a vacation hanging around.
> Upon her arrival, the phone did ring,
> I had planned to do not a thing.

> The chief dispatcher was there to say,
> "Merry Christmas, Vera. It's Carlton today.
> Like a babe in the wilderness, I did go,
> To second trick, hoping it'd be mighty slow.

> But found a job with responsibility and trains galore.
> Thank goodness it wasn't one day more.
> The agent was nice as he good be,
> Collecting overtime as a fee.

> The switch crew's coffee was really good,
> But train 623 by the station stood.
> With Lee at the fires, and the dispatcher on hand,

Bob and Roland helped out, since I'm such a ham.

The clock struck 12 and Williams left,
The depot was there, and so were the rest.

Putting aside humor, I remember one night we had a terrible accident. A Milwaukee diesel was coming into the yard, and the engineer had fallen asleep. The train was going too fast, and it rear-ended an NP train, causing 58 cars to pile up. The engine ended up on the highway killing one yardman and injuring another. The brakeman on the NP lost his leg. The engineer of the Milwaukee diesel came into the station, took a piece of paper, and wrote out his resignation right there on the spot, because he knew he was going to be fired. No one was ever given a second chance when there was such an error.

I learned this lesson very early in my training. There was no way to "pass the buck" with this deadly accident.

Rush City, Minnesota

Station name: Rush City
Division: Lake Superior, main line, third subdivision
Station #: L99
Telegrapher's call: RC

Many times, we would have heavy loads on the railroad. Montgomery Wards had a load of catalogs that arrived in Rush City. Now, many people during that time couldn't wait to see those catalogs, but I had a different opinion of them when they were being loaded. Each bag weighed at least 50 pounds.

One whole week, I had to unload these bags of catalogs and sort them for their destination. Some stayed in Rush City. That was a relief. The mailman could take it from there, but the rest had to be transferred to another baggage cart and loaded onto the train going to Grantsburg and surrounding areas.

The first night, a policeman helped me unload the mail, saying, "Vera, that's too heavy for you."

I agreed. The next night, there was no policeman or any help. When asked why not, he said, "I can't come down to help you. The work's too hard!"

But I was young and agile in those days, so I got the work done. The next day, I got a baby buffalo. Now, that was hard work.

One of the worst jobs I had was a load of chickens. I discovered that if you come into the warehouse, and a load of chickens gets loose, you have a *real* problem. Good-bye, Rush City!

DU at Duluth, Minnesota

Station name: Duluth
Division: Lake Superior, Duluth and Superior terminals, first subdivision
Station #: Main terminal
Telegrapher's call: DU

I'd come a long way. Perhaps the ultimate job for a telegrapher was to be assigned to the Duluth office to work with the Chief Dispatcher. He was located on the highest floor of the Union Station. This beautiful French Chateauesque building was built in 1892, becoming the bustling hub of activity for much of the 20th century. By 1910, seven railroads dispatched over 50 trains a day from Duluth. I had to take many messages all shift long. I'd report these messages to the dispatcher, who had to reply. Send and receive was the whole day's assignment. I worked this station on the weekends, as I taught school during the week.

Duluth Union Station (Lake Superior Railroad Museum)

An Immigrants' waiting room served as a small Ellis Island for the region's newest arrivals to await their connections. During times of war, regiments of soldiers marched down Superior Street to board trains for service. Fortunately, the Duluth Union Station has been saved. Today, it's known as the Lake Superior Railroad Museum of Transportation and Industry.

Perhaps the very highest position is the Chief Dispatcher, who is usually very experienced and well-respected among the telegraphers. It is the most difficult and demanding position of the railroad. A dispatcher must make snap decisions, especially in crisis situations. The responsibilities include overseeing all train operations and personnel on the division. He must know the location and movement of all train traffic, the types of trains and the consist (number and description of cars in the train). Then he plans where to have trains meet on single tracks, places one on a sidetrack based on the train's length and time schedule, and solves all problems as they arrive.

The Chief Dispatcher usually comes up through the ranks, so he knows every aspect of railroading. Administration appoints the Chief Dispatcher, instead of posting this position for seniority bidding. An applicant is tested rigorously on their knowledge of railroading. The buck stops here! If anything happens, the Chief Dispatcher is responsible.

As busy as the Chief Dispatcher was, his authority meant nothing to my mother. When he called to give me my next job assignment, Mother would answer, "Call later. She's sleeping."

Of course, in my household, Mother was our Chief Dispatcher. All railroads were represented. My step-father was an agent on the Chicago Northwestern, my brother, Lyle, was a telegrapher on the Soo Line, and I worked for the Northern Pacific.

Having full respect for her authority, the dispatcher replied, "Have Vera call me when she wakes up."

Railroading requires an exact time for scheduling. For everyone to operate on the same time schedule, the automatic time clock was located in the Duluth office. At 11 a.m. every day, all stations set their clocks at exactly the same minute as the master clock. The clock automatically ticked off the time over every telegraph instrument for all stations to check their clock's accuracy.

In this era of railroading, passenger trains had rights over freight trains. Today they are the reverse, leading to poorer passenger service.

Poplar, Wisconsin

Station name: Poplar
Division: Lake Superior, main line, first subdivision
Station #: 48
Telegrapher's call: AR

Being a small farming community, there were only a few weigh freight trains that came through Poplar's station on a weekly basis. But, this town is mainly renowned for being the home of Major Richard Bong, America's most successful flying ace of World War II. As a fighter pilot, he protected the skies of the South Pacific from Japanese attacks by shooting down 40 enemy planes.

I was familiar with this area because I went to college with Richard's sister, Jerry, and I often visited her at the Bong farm. My brother, Lyle, knew Richard Bong's wife, Marge, very well. We were very sad when Richard died at the age of 24 while he was testing the first Lockheed fighter plane on the same day that the atomic bomb was dropped on Hiroshima. He usually flew a P-38 fighter plane, and there was a replica of his airplane outside of the depot in Poplar.

Richard Bong's P38 with Marge's Photo

Many people lost their jobs in this area, so people would come to the depot to sign up for unemployment. This was a new area for me, so I had to learn the proper procedure for filing the form. Fortunately, my stepfather, Axel Nordholm, had worked 50 years on the Railroad and was a great help offering me guidance in this and many other areas of my telegraph career. I thought, "This isn't such a bad idea, in case I have to file for unemployment some day."

Cloquet, Minnesota

Station name: Cloquet
Division: Lake Superior, Cloquet branch, fifth subdivision
Station #: LC7
Telegrapher's call: CQ

I went to Cloquet two different times. The first time was in the winter. It was bitter cold. I had visited the city before but never knew where the station was located. So when the dispatcher called me to work, it was imperative that I find the depot. Having some difficulty, I followed the tracks until I discovered the large structure, which didn't look like any of the smaller depots that I was familiar with on the NP.

Cloquet NP Depot

I went through the front door, and found four or five men working at the front desks. One of them came forward. "How may I help you?" he asked.

I answered, "Are you looking for a relief supervisory agent?"

He retorted, "Some guy by the name of Williams is coming."

My response was, "I'm it." Upon that statement, every head shot up. This was going to be my team. They escorted me into my private office. One man opened my mail. Another man called up to the paper mill. I hadn't the vaguest idea what I was supposed to do, but the others didn't seem to notice and continued to do my work. I simply supervised.

One employee had to garnish a customer's wages. He completed the form and collected the fee of 50 cents. He handed me the fee saying, "This is your commission."

I replied, "No, you keep it. I didn't do the work." Promptly at 10 a.m., another employee entered my office. "We usually have coffee and rolls in the warehouse. Would you care to join us?"

I felt after all of this hard work that I was badly in need of a break, so I joined them.

At 2 p.m., the Chief Dispatcher called me and said, "It's snowing rather heavily. You might want to leave work early."

The pay for this rigorous day was a whole $25. This sure beat my regular pay of 85 cents per hour.

That following summer, much to my surprise, the men specifically asked for Williams to replace the agent while he went on vacation. They said, "They wanted me because I was so well-qualified for the job." I gladly obliged. That was the highest paying position I obtained in my railroad experience. Too bad it was so short-lived.

Brule, Wisconsin

Station name: Brule
Division: Lake Superior, main line, first subdivision
Station #: 36
Telegrapher's call: BX

The famous Brule River flows 50 miles north of Lake Superior. It became a famous tourist attraction because it's a haven for anglers. Several presidents traveled on the Northern Pacific to the town of Brule to fish trout in the river and to enjoy the spectacular view. In fact, President Coolidge's summer White House was in Superior, Wisconsin. The city built an arch over the highway to the entrance of Superior in honor of his visit.

Brule became a favorite spot for other presidents of the U.S. to relax, especially Presidents Ulysses S. Grant, Dwight D. Eisenhower, Herbert Hoover, and Harry Truman. They rode in a private coach from Superior to Brule.

The depot in Brule, although a small building, was a good place to work because the agent could collect extra fees for unloading express for businessman and ambassadors who had homes along the river.

Brule was also known for its excellent trees through the area. One morning, I arrived early at the station to find two irate loggers in the waiting room, each claiming they had ordered a pulp car. However, there was only one available on the sidetrack. This presented a dilemma.

I hadn't ordered any cars for either of the loggers, so which one would get it? The agent who had ordered the pulp car originally wasn't available.

After an angry exchange, I came up with a solution. I said, "The first one who gets a stick of wood into that car gets it, and I'll order another one for in the morning."

With that, both men dashed out of the depot towards the car. Oh, what a fight there was. Fists were flying. One eventually returned with a bloody nose to order his car for in the morning. Brute strength has its merits in Brule.

Cromwell, Minnesota

Station name: Cromwell
Division: Lake Superior, main line, second subdivision
Station #: 108
Telegrapher's call: CM

Cromwell was predominantly a Finnish community. People did everything very hard there. They worked hard, played hard, fought hard, and drank hard. During the war, the railroad paid Mexican workers to replace the ballast on the tracks. That means they put crushed rock on the track. The workers lived in railroad cars near the depot. Because they weren't used to getting any money, they were suspicious of one another, and they fought over everything.

The station down the track had many workers who were American Indians. The Mexican workers would visit their neighboring town to visit the Indian women. This didn't go over very well, so the Indian workers would retaliate, by coming down to the Cromwell depot and dumping bullets into the waiting room's pot-belly stove. What a big bang. The first time I heard it, I nearly jumped out of my skin. I hated working at the depot, especially on Saturday nights when the men became inebriated. We almost had another Indian War and had to call the sheriff to keep these two parties apart.

On paydays, the agent was the paymaster. The funds arrived in a wax-sealed envelope. I'd count out the appropriate amount of money for each employee and place it into a stack on the long table. Thankfully, the road crew foreman came into the depot to identify each employee as they received their pay. I found it rather difficult, as it seemed to me that every crewman had the last name of Garcia. I'd call out the name Jose Garcia, then Manuel Garcia, Jesus Garcia, Miguel Garcia, and the list went on and on. This group of Garcia's did not trust one another. They would even lock up their shoes at night with padlocks because they were afraid someone would steal them. Needless to say, payday was not my favorite day of the week.

However, I did learn to appreciate my Garcia's when it came to mealtime. There was only one restaurant in town, which was an old remodeled streetcar. All they served was eggs, eggs, eggs. Since it was during the War, no one had meat. I ate so many eggs that I could have clucked.

One fine day, I was invited down to the railroad crew car to have coffee with the cook. I found out that he served real meat. So, from then on, I'd go down and eat with the crew. It was a real treat compared to eating at the restaurant. It appears the NP had a better ration card than I had.

When I got to Cromwell, as usual, I had to find my own lodging. I stayed out at a farm where the couple practically adopted me. I used to ride in a Model T Ford. We would drive to the next town to deliver the milk each day. The rumble seat was removed to hold the two milk cans. The driver would fire up the Ford, and his wife scooted into the car. I sat next to her. We went all of 20 miles per hour, while his wife yelled, "Slow down, you're driving too fast."

I guess the couple liked me because I also helped him hay. His wife always said, "If my husband dies, will you come back to see me."

I said, "Sure," but I never did. It's 70 years later, so he must be dead by now.

Another time, I was in Cromwell when they sent me a student operator. Unlike *my* vast orientation experience, I was to train the new recruit. He happened to be of Irish descent. Of course, it would have to be on a day when we had to deal with several messages sent through Western Union.

Earlier in the day, a young lad had attempted suicide and didn't succeed the task. He was transported to Duluth via ambulance for emergency care. His parents came to the depot to notify several relatives of the situation. The body of the telegram would remain the same, but the heading was individualized based on who received the message.

I showed my young recruit the Western Union guide on this procedure. According to the rulebook, the body of the letter would only need to be sent once, while each individual receiving the message was listed. Unfortunately, the Western Union Operator had his own protocols on how to send multiple messages. The operator stated that every message must repeat the body of the telegram, which took forever. I fought with the Western Union Operator up until I heard the whistle of a train.

Looking out the window, I saw that the passenger train was coming from Duluth. When it stopped at our station, the conductor was standing in the doorway of the baggage car. He said very seriously, "Get your express cart. We have a body."

I replied, "The express cart is full of freight."

He replied, "Get your hand cart, then."

This young recruit went into the warehouse and pulled out a hand cart, very cautiously. He's wondering how this cart is going to be of any use since it's so low to the ground. We both made the assumption that the body was that of the young lad who attempted suicide. The baggage man pushed the rough box to the edge of the car and started to tip it to the cart.

The young recruit yelled, "You can't tip him on his head!"

With that, the conductor exclaimed, "Ah, he's nothing but a dumb Irishman!"

I can still remember the look on the kid's face. The baggage man was laughing, but we didn't join him until we discovered the rough box was empty. Never assume!

On a lighter side, I remember handing up a train order for a meet at McGregor. The engineer received the order and continued forward. On handing it up to the conductor at the rear end of the train, I accidentally hooked his order onto two cars before the caboose.

Technically, the conductor should have pulled the air brakes to stop the train and receive the order. However, going at that speed would have caused quite a delay. So, knowing that the head end had the order, I stretched the rule and waved the conductor on by saying, "Keep going, keep going, keep going." I later found out that the conductor walked up the two cars and retrieved the order that was stuck to the freight car.

The next day on the return trip, the conductor of the freight train threw off a message to me wrapped around a Hershey Bar with a whole sheet saying, "Keep going, keep going." He saw the humor in my mistake and appreciated that he didn't have to stop the train.

Aitkin, Minnesota

Station name: Aitkin
Division: Lake Superior, main line, second subdivision
Station #: 150
Telegrapher's call: KN

Five women worked in our division on the Northern Pacific. They were very skilled, fast, and efficient. Perhaps the only place that they were not qualified was in the tower positions where my father worked, due to the difficulty in pulling the heavy levers. Women were restricted there.

Aitkin Northern Pacific Depot

Rarely, did I find anyone who discriminated against me, but in Aitkin, Minnesota, I ran into this conductor who really didn't like women. He felt that women were incompetent, lightweight, and ignorant. I'm not even sure that he was pleased that his wife had the right to vote.

The conductor stepped off the caboose, went into the depot and stated, "Throw the switch as we go by, so I can make the hill to Carlton."

My answer was, "No!"

"Do as I say!" he snapped and turned to leave.

"I can't, because a switchman can time slip me." A time slip means the railroad would have to pay the switchman for his assigned work and pay me as well for the same job. Unions don't like people doing another person's job.

That stopped the conductor, cold. He slammed the door as he left the depot muttering a few words I'd never heard before. I wouldn't doubt that he's still fuming!

While I worked in Aitkin, I stayed at a rooming house where there were only men, except for me. Most of them were loggers and local labors. At suppertime, we were all seated at a long table. There were tons of food. I'd never seen so many mashed potatoes in my life! The men quietly waited while I was served first. Then, all hell broke loose as the food was violently devoured. I was lucky to have my share first because there were no seconds.

One man caused a great consternation when he picked up the bowl of gravy, thinking it was soup, and ate the whole bowlful.

When the potatoes arrived, the men asked, "Where's the gravy?"

The cook said, "I put it on the table, but somebody ate it!"

All eyes turned to the person who ate the soup. There was one man in trouble in Aitkin that night.

White Bear Lake, Minnesota

Station name: White Bear Lake
Division: Lake Superior, main line, third subdivision
Station #: L141
Telegrapher's call: WB

White Bear Lake Northern Pacific Depot Museum

Sometimes, one didn't stay very long at a job, but my experience in White Bear Lake takes the cake. I received notice from the dispatcher to go to White Bear Lake, Minnesota. When I arrived, the agent told me my duties and then took me over to the hotel where the last operator had stayed. Opening the door to the room, I could still see the imprint on the mattress of the last person who'd slept there.

The maid hadn't finished cleaning the room, yet. She looked tired as if she'd had a rough night. I found it odd when I saw a rope hanging in front of the window. I asked the maid, "What's the rope for?"

She replied, "Well, that's for an emergency. You just break the window, grab the rope, and swing out then drop to the ground." I looked out the second-floor window and thought, *I hope there's no fire tonight.*

Realizing that I was staying in a vastly improved room, complete with a fire escape, I considered myself lucky. I really couldn't complain, because the last room I had stayed in at another town had an iron bed with the legs sitting in coffee cans of kerosene. When I asked the maid why the legs were sitting in coffee cans, she replied, "It prevents infestation of bedbugs getting into the mattress." Thinking back, I remembered that there was no rope in that room. It was sure fortunate that I didn't smoke.

The maid finished cleaning my room. I went to work at 4 p.m. until it was time to go back to the hotel for the evening meal. When I sat down to eat, there was a massive amount of potatoes, gravy, and a huge hunk of meat. Dessert was about three quarts of fresh strawberries. After I had my fill, the owner remarked, "You don't eat much compared to the last operator! Now, remember where I placed the key, so you can get back in after you finish your shift at midnight."

I guess that everyone must go to bed at eight o'clock in that town.

Upon returning to the depot, I received a notice that I had been bumped. That meant another telegrapher was taking my place tomorrow, and I was to take the early train back to Duluth as soon as my shift was over. I didn't even get to sleep in that lovely bed. I returned long enough to grab my suitcase and catch the train back home.

Brainerd, Minnesota

Station name: Brainerd
Division: Lake Superior, main line, second subdivision
Station #: 177
Telegrapher's call: B

While working at Brainerd, I had to reorient myself to managing a larger station. It was one of the biggest communities that I worked in during my career. Being a main tourist attraction area with many lakes and the famous Paul Bunyan and Babe, the Blue Ox, there were many passengers. This brick station was elegant compared to the wooden structures where I usually worked. It even had indoor plumbing instead of an outhouse.

The first duty of every operator was to check the cash drawer at the beginning of his or her shift. My colleague, Loren Sloan, gave a good description. He stated, "The cash drawer was located below the ticket window and could be opened by pressing finger keys located under and towards the front of the cash drawer. A working fund of usually $10 was always to be kept on hand for making change. Many an Agent over the years were dismissed for borrowing from the $10 cash fund and being caught by an unexpected visiting auditor."

Stations handling sizable amounts of money were equipped with a small metal safe issued by the "American Express Company," the predecessor of the Railway Express Agency.

The ticket case was located on the shelf next to the ticket window. Nearby hung baggage checks on individual strings to be placed on the passenger's luggage before they were loaded into the baggage car. It was the operator's responsibility to load the luggage onto the express cart before the train arrived. Prior to the arrival, the loaded express cart was spotted onto the platform where the baggage car would be located.

When the train stopped at the depot, the operator jumped up onto the express cart and loaded the bags into the baggage car. Then the agent pulled the cart forward to the mail car to load and receive the mail. There were several express carts in Brainerd as there was a lot of mail.

Also, metal car seals were hanging from a metal ring hooked on a bent nail on the wall of the depot next to the baggage claim tickets. Each seal was made of a long strip of metal with a unique number etched into it. Before and after each freight train, I'd pick up the ring and hang it over my arm, and then I'd grab the seal record book and head out to the railroad cars. All seal numbers had to be recorded as they were placed or removed from a car, along with other pertinent information.

Recent railroad cars delivered by the freight train were already sealed. I walked up to each car door and broke the seal, recorded the number in the book, and it was now ready to be unloaded. When the car was reloaded, I would remove a metal car seal from the ring, record the number of the seal into the book, and the train would pick up the car on its next run.

Hinckley, Minnesota

Station name: Hinckley
Division: Lake Superior, main line, third subdivision
Station #: L76
Telegrapher's call: HN
National Register of Historic Places: Building #73000992

I worked in Hinckley, which has become a historical museum. The station, originally named Central Station, was renamed Hinckley after the great fire of 1894. The original NP depot burned to the ground during that fire.

The new depot built living quarters above to accommodate the telegrapher, as many of these small towns at that time didn't provide an area for their operators. I relieved the agent at Hinckley, but I didn't stay in his quarters above the depot.

The fire was long before my time, but the events run deep in the town, and anyone who worked at the station learned of that fateful event.

A young telegrapher, Thomas G. Dunn, remained loyal at his post even after hearing the devastating news that a massive fire annihilated the nearby town of Pokegama., now called Brook Park.

As the fire approached Hinckley, Dunn stayed at his telegraph, calling for help and sending words of warning along the wires. He knew that Engineer James Root was on a Southbound Passenger Train, Engine 69, and refused to leave the depot in hopes to warn him of impending danger.

Dunn gave his life saving his town's people. The final words he transmitted were, "I think I've stayed too long."[1]

Unfortunately, he succumbed to the fire. The next day, Dunn's father found Tommy's body by Grindstone River.

Agent Thomas G. Dunn

If it hadn't been for the railroads and their employees, who bravely saved hundreds of people, many more would have died during the disaster. Other heroes that day were three engineers, William Best, Edward Berry, and James Root.[2] There were also two conductors, H. D. Powers and Tom Sullivan, and Porter John Blair. All did their part to save lives, even transporting passengers in burning rescue trains to get them to safety.[3]

There were 418 men, women, and children who perished in the Great Hinckley Fire. Some believe it was closer to 800. The fire not only destroyed Hinckley, but it also burned out five other communities: Pokegama, Mission Creek, Partridge, Miller (a station nine miles north of Hinckley, which no longer exists), and Sandstone.[4]

Here's the detailed story of this devastating event.

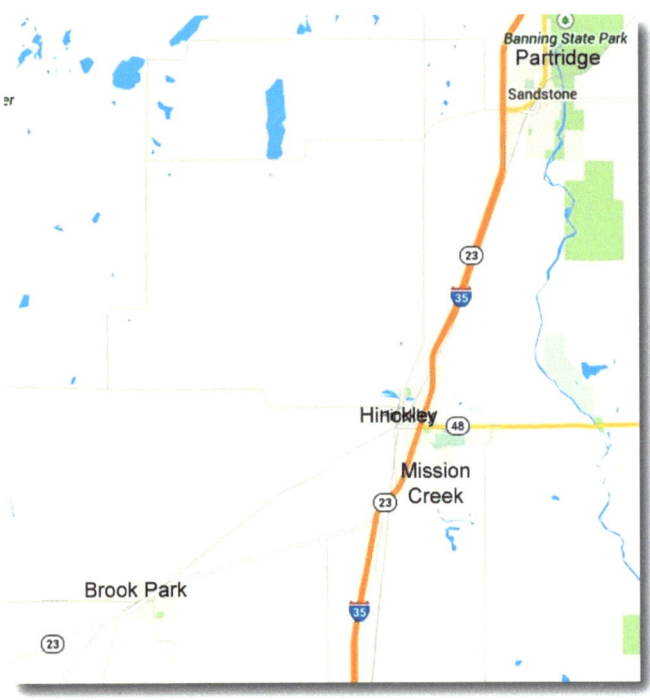

Map of Towns Devastated in Hinckley Fire

In the early 1800s, this territory was home to the Ojibwa Indians and later the Chippewa. Over time, logging camps, sawmills, and railroads spread over the land. Small townships soon followed.

Between May and September 1894, only two inches of rain fell during the entire four months. It was the driest summer of the past 128 years.[5] Fires plagued the area all summer long. Hardwoods, giant pines, and swampland were primed for a disaster.

Every week or so, the Northern Pacific section men had to fight a blaze along the rail line to keep the right of way clear. They even helped neighbors to battle frequent bursts of flames. Farmers lost tons of hay, but there were no reports of any damaged buildings. The wheat withered, and the corn dried up making great tinder. Loggers frequently left wood and debris, making for good fuel.

Then around noon on September 1, 1894, a thick cloud of dust and ashes blew into these small villages. By two o'clock, a powerful wind whipped up, and it was like the sky rained fire. The temperature spiked, trapping gases in the air then they'd explode. Flames leapt into the sky. It seemed as if they grew legs and sprinted 1,500 to 2,000 feet per step.[6] The fire raged across 480 miles and burned 350,000 acres.[7]

Flames Overtook the Area

Pokegama

Pokegama's population was 135 people. The day dawned as a hazy blue smoke filtered the air giving a mellow glow of sunlight. But wait, it wasn't the sun. It was a raging forest fire. The townsfolk had battled small, smoldering boughts of brush for the past three months. All noticed the fires were getting more frequent and coming closer to town, but they had a good fire brigade. Surely they could cope with this blaze.

Alas, the heavens opened up with sparks hopping from one house to the next. In a matter of moments flames ate everything in its path. There was no time to save one's belongings. There was only time to run.

A railroad bridge ran over a small pond of water, which ran about 15 feet deep at its center. This was the town's only respite. People came from every direction. Too deep to stand, the people clustered along the water's edge. As the fire closed in, it drove the people deeper into the pool. Splashing each other to keep cool, they finally moved deeper until only their heads could be seen as they'd bob up for a mouthful of air so thick it choked them. For two hours, they stayed in the pool as the town burned around them. Finally, they crowded into two railroad cars left untouched by the fire. Even so, 23 people died.

Outside Pokegama, near Shadridge Creek, Chief Wacaouta and his band of Chippewa Indians perished, leaving another 23 dead.

Mission Creek

Six miles to the east was Mission Creek. According to records, there were 26 homes, a schoolhouse, blacksmith shop, a small sawmill, hotel, and a general store in the little hamlet.

People ran for their lives and gathered at the store. The owner telegraphed for a train to come to town to rescue them. The railroad ran through the heart of the pine country and provided transportation for logging camps.

While the people waited for the train, smoke filled the area making it hard to breathe. It was a black as night, even though it was barely four o'clock in the afternoon. The whole town was on fire. The people retreated to the rear of the store. When the building caught fire, everyone ran outside to a potato patch and lay on the ground.[8]

A work train from Pine City managed to cut through the flames and rescued the survivors. The town lay in ruins. The survivors were fortunate.

Hinkley

By two p.m., the cyclone of fire raged into Hinckley and started a few buildings ablaze on the outskirts of town. Firefighters rang the alarm. They quickly strung out all 2,000 feet of fire hose. Unable to control the flames, the fire chief put out an urgent notice for Rush City to send another 600 feet of hose.

Flames Overtook the Area

The wind refused to let up. A wall of cracking, hissing flames roared up Main Street from the south like a hurricane. By 2:15, the town was beyond saving. Unable to fight the fire, the brave firemen climbed on their horses, headed into the heavy smoke, ashes, and flames to evacuate whomever they could.

In desperation, they called, "Abandon you homes! Run to the river! Go to the gravel pit! Get to the eastern depot!"

Many people clustered at the gravel pit, others in the river, but the fire was on a deadly course. No one was safe. People left everything and ran, but many couldn't run fast enough. Others fled on horseback, but they too were engulfed in the flames, most suffocated.

Great Northern Rescue Train - Engineer Edward Barry, Conductor H. D. Powers & Engineer William Best

At 2:40 p.m., a Great Northern Railroad freight train, Engine 105 barreled into town. Edward Barry was the engineer. "Everything was on fire as I drove into Hinckley. The heat and smoke were intense, almost to suffocation. Engineer William Best and Conductor Powers sat in Engine 24, another freight train which had been sidetracked waiting for the 3:25 southbound passenger train causing them to await orders. According to our rules, I had to side track the freight train and wait, too."

Conductor H. D. Powers

It is a rule of the railroad that when two trains must join forces, the conductor of senior rank takes charge. It's was also a rule that freight trains must wait on a sidetrack until a passenger train passes when using the same track.

Fortunately, Conductor Powers was in command and had the foresight to put that rule behind him during this emergency. Powers consulted with Engineer Best of the sidetracked train and had him couple the two trains together adding on three box cars, a caboose, and five passenger coaches to the two engines.[9]

Engineers Best and Barry worked together to form an emergency rescue train and pulled it up to the depot. However, they weren't in total agreement. Barry wanted to load quickly and get out of town before the fire socked them in.

Engineer William Best

Engineer Edward Barry

William Best saw the people pouring from the streets fighting to make it to the depot. He consulted with Conductor Powers.

When Barry gave two short whistle blasts, the signal to back up the train to leave, Conductor Powers refused to release the train. Instead, Engineer Best set the air brakes of his engine to hold tight so more people could board the train and escape town. Best held a firm grip on the air brakes for 45 minutes. By then, they'd loaded 276 panic-stricken town folks, and the streets were aflame. The air was too thick to breathe.

Barry was afraid everyone on board would suffocate. Unable to wait any longer, Powers agreed to head back to Duluth.

Best released the air brakes, and Barry moved out of town through ash and flame. By the time the train was about seven miles from Hinckley, the air finally improved.

After the train had left the station, about 70 more people found their way to the gravel pit. The water hole was two to three acres across and dropped to about twenty to thirty feet into a cold pool of water. Many domestic animals were already in the pit. All made it through the fire without injury. About 200 more people made it to Skunk Lake.

Sandstone and Partridge

When the rescue train reached Sandstone, more people poured onto the train. The conductors didn't worry about tickets. The train crew helped everyone aboard as fast as they could.

"The bridge is on fire!" someone screamed as Barry pulled out of Sandstone.

He slowed to assess the situation. Indeed, the bridge over Kettle River was ablaze.

Engineer Best blasted his horn and leaned out the engine window giving the highball sign, which is a fist in the air rotating in a circle. He yelled, "For God's sake go. You can cross now, but the bridge will burn down in five minutes."

With no time to turn around, Barry threw the throttle wide open in reverse to escape the fire and relied on two brakemen to flag him safely across the burning bridge. As the train passed, the bridge soon crumbled into the water, but the train made it over the river and kept barreling up the tracks.

The brakemen raced through the train and climbed the swaying railcars. They held tight to the brake wheels and cranked with all their might. Then they had to hop across one car to reach the next and set its brake to slow the train. Every man on the crew worked together.

They continued to rescue people along the way between Sandstone and Partridge, but the train had been through a lot. Many soot-faced passengers suffered from coughing fits. The rescue train stopped for twenty-minute at Partridge, which was six miles north of Sandstone.

It was the first chance to deliver water to the passengers, and Conductor Powers made his way through the aisles trying to make everyone as comfortable as possible. It was Powers call to link the two trains, and without a team effort, hundreds of more lives would have been lost.

The train made it to West Superior, where the passengers got off the train, exhausted and hungry, but safe. The smoke burned Engineer Barry's eyes, and by the end of the trip he was almost blind.

Engine No. 69 - James Root, Conductor Sullivan & Porter John Blair - Rescue at Skunk Lake

The Northern Pacific was very busy that day. Another heroic train pulled out of Duluth going southbound around two o'clock. It was the passenger train that Agent Dunn was waiting for.

The engineer of Engine No. 69 was James Root. The train consisted of one combination car, one coach, and two chair cars. As Root headed toward Carlton, smoke grew thicker. There were 150 passengers aboard, who became increasingly alarmed as the train roared down the tracks. Flames leapt at them from both sides of the train. The heat was insufferable, and people had difficulty breathing.

As they approached Hinckley, the train passed by Skunk Lake, where many people flagged down the train. Hundreds of people climbed aboard, some layered in soot, while others were soaking wet as they fled the fire. Soon the train had picked up nearly 200 refugees as they headed into Hinckley

The conductor, Tom Sullivan, listened to the passenger's panicked stories, and then he saw the flames blasting toward them like a twister. Fire surrounded them. Sullivan decided they couldn't enter Hinckley and to run the train back to Skunk Lake. He dashed up to the engine to stop the train.

Conductor Thomas Sullivan

The train screeched to a halt as Engineer Root reversed direction back through the blaze. Smoke came through the vents, danced along the tops of the cars, and crept through the windows. Soon the rear coach was on fire. Terror ripped through the passengers as they ran for the front of the train away from the blaze. It got so hot, the windows shattered from their frames. Passengers went wild.[10]

Engineer Root's Engine 69 -
Made Last Trainload of Survivors Out of Hinckley

The train erupted into flames. Even though Engineer Root had second and third-degree burns, he stayed at the throttle and kept that train going in reverse for a full five miles to Skunk Lake. His burned hands so swollen; they were nearly twice their normal size.

Porter Blair raced through the train with a fire extinguisher dousing burning clothing and yelling, "Get down. Keep your head down." As the train reached the swamp water, people screamed and jumped from the train. Some leapt through windows and landed in the mud. As people climbed from the train at Skunk Lake, Porter John Blair assisted them. He made repeated trips back to the burning coaches to rescue children.

Engineer James Root   *Porter John Blair*

Without regard for his own welfare, Porter Blair was the last one to leave the doomed train. He only left when he was certain all the passengers were off. People laid in the mud and water for hours, trying to breathe without suffocating. As the fire died out, everyone was saved, except for one person who had wandered away from the rest.

Hinckley lost 197 people in the fire. As I said earlier, the railroad rebuilt the depot, and it is now a museum.

Hinckley Station Now a Museum

Iron River, Wisconsin

Station name: Iron River
Division: Lake Superior, main line, first subdivision
Station #: 28
Telegrapher's call: RV

As a telegrapher, I worked as a relief agent at Iron River one summer, while the regular agent went on vacation. Because the division was relatively small, the local traffic was limited. The weigh freight would come once a week to load and unload products for the local businesses. They would spot the empty cars for loading and pick up those already loaded. The job was fairly easy, and I'd take a leisurely visit to town while the crew frequently stopped to take lunch.

Iron River Northern Pacific depot – 1944

I worked at this location several times. There is one story, in particular, which I recall. One day, the conductor of the weigh freight came into the depot and reported that there was a broken rail along the tracks. I thought it was important to send that message to the dispatcher, so he could put out a slow order. It seemed like my first priority. As always, safety first!

As I was sending the order, the conductor stormed back into the depot, shouting, "What are you doing? Your job is to be out there in the warehouse to help with the load."

The red hair flew as my ire grew. Dashing out into the warehouse, I moved past four perfectly capable men and exclaimed, "Okay, you guys step back. I'm here to do a man's work!" There was a ten-foot roll of spun wool lying on the floor of the warehouse. I hefted that huge bag of wool and threw it across the platform, into the open door of the freight car.

Evidently, it impressed the men because they guffawed at the conductor. This was the same man who had chided me for not throwing the switch at Aitkin.

The conductor slinked out of the warehouse, and I didn't see him again for the rest of the day, which was fine with me.

Later, I heard through the grapevine that he said, "You know what? I don't believe that women should be working on the railroad, but Williams is different." I had proven my point. Women can do a man's work!

Whenever I came to town, I ate at the infamous Vasha Restaurant. It was just across the street from where I was boarding for the night. My landlady, Mrs. Pettingill, escorted me to my room and told me to get a good night's sleep.

Unfortunately, the restaurant caught fire during the night. Unbelievable to my landlady, I slept soundly even though the fire alarm was screaming, and the townsfolk congregated practically outside my window. She wanted to wake me up in the worst way, but she knew that I needed my sleep.

Lo and behold, when I finally woke up and pulled up the shade, the restaurant was gone. There was only a heap of ashes. It was the most disastrous event this community ever had, and Mrs. Pettingill couldn't believe that I slept through the whole thing.

Another big event of a different nature happened on a Saturday while everyone was at the dance having a wonderful time. I received a telegraph message from the U.S. government for the mother of my best friend. It stated that her son was missing in action while serving his country.

According to regulations, I had to deliver this type of message before 11 p.m. Not wanting her mother to be alone when she got the message, I went to the town dance to find my friend, so she could accompany me to her home.

In the past, the agent was alone when delivering messages from the military, but the stress of the message caused the recipient varying degrees of emotional stress, even to point of dying of a heart attack. As World War II continued, and more of these dreaded messages were sent home to the parents, the ministers of each faith volunteered to go with the agent to deliver these messages.

Being a small community, news traveled fast, and the dance ended immediately. I found this was the worst task I was ever assigned. During the war, these messages were not uncommon. They were very long and detailed. One never wanted to make a mistake. This war experience remains etched in my mind forever.

When I graduated from college in 1948, I accepted a teaching position in Portage, Wisconsin, but I continued to work summers and vacations on the railroad. After three years, the railroad needed my services on a full-time basis and insisted on my return, or I would lose my seniority rights.

Wanting to change teaching positions, I decided instead to return to railroading, so that I wouldn't lose my seniority. However, as I was sitting in the Iron River Depot, shoveling coal into the pot-bellied stove, I wondered, "What am I doing here with a college degree?" It was the middle of October, and it was getting very cold. The men were returning from military service, and they wanted their jobs back.

The tasks assigned to me by the agent were to take care of what trains came through and file the tariffs in the warehouse. I took one look at those tariffs and realized they hadn't been filed in 20 years. The dust had accumulated, but I took the task seriously for the first night. I realized on the next night that the results weren't happening fast enough. Taking a closer look, I found a simpler solution. I began filing those tariffs directly into the stove. Boy, did I keep warm that night. Now that I'd completed the task that I had been assigned to, I was finally ready for a new adventure. A woman has the right to change her mind.

Women on the Railroad

At the time the railroad hired me, they were short of telegraphers because many of the men were drafted into the service. In order to fill the positions, the railroad resorted to hiring women.

Much of the passenger traffic at that time was soldiers in full uniform heading to the west coast for basic training. In Superior, it was not unusual to see, on any given night, the evening train filled with recruits heading to Chicago. They were going to a military base for their physicals. The station brimmed with emotion as the platform filled with families, girlfriends, and loved ones waving good-bye to the soldiers as trains pulled out of town. For many, this would be the last time they'd ever see their son, husband, or father.

To accommodate the heavy passenger traffic, every car owned by the railroad was put into use. There were gaslights and a stove in each car. Some of these cars are still used today for old-time movies.

As an employee, I would ride the train on my pass. Many times, I had to give up my seat to a paying passenger. Then, I would go into the baggage car and sit on a milk can, which was sometimes very entertaining, as I'd share lunch with the baggage man. We'd greet other employees as we passed each station.

The war provided women a means to get us into the man's world. When the war hit, the women stepped up to the plate and without complaint. A woman got a man's pay, did a man's work, and worked the same schedule as a man. We even got a vacation and a pension.

The attitude of the worker has changed. Today you work at something, but that wasn't the case with the railroad. The loyalty of the worker was obvious. I worked *at* the University, but I worked *for* the railroad.

If we could ride the rails as we did in the past, what a glorious day it would be.

I spent my retirement riding the rails wherever I could. I loved to give talks at Rusty Rails meetings, schools, and the University.

Unfortunately today, passenger trains in the U.S. have gone by the wayside. I miss the smoke of the steam, power of the diesel, and the lonesome wail of the whistle.

By Gone Days

Author Unknown

Along a rusty railroad track
I stepped from tie to tie
And let my memory wander back
To days now long gone by.
An ancient depot came in view
Where weeds were growing tall,
Inside the spacious baggage room
Old milk cans lined the wall.
The scroll work on the door post told
Of splendor dimmed by time,
When Iron Horses pulled their trains
Along the railroad line.
The sun was fading from the sky
As I looked down the rail,
A lonely signal stood its watch
But all to no avail.

Notes

1. "Great Hinckley Fire of 1894." *Hinckley.gov*. 18 Dec. 2014. Web. <http://www.hinckley.govoffice2.com/>.

2. "Great Hinckley Fire of 1894."

3. *Hinckley Fire Museum*. 2014. Web. <http://hinckleyfiremuseum.com/index.html>.

4. *Hinckley Fire Museum*.

5. McNally, Janet. "The Hinckley Fire of 1894." *Tamarack lamb&wool.* 1997. Web. <http://www.tamaracksheep.com/Hinckley%20Fire.html>.

6. "On This Day in Weather History with Mark Mancuso: The Great Hinckley Fire (Saturday, September 1st, 1894)" *AccuWeather.com*. Web. <https://www.youtube.com/watch?v=z5Bzg4nztDk>.

7. "The Great Hinckley Fire." *Rising Legion Films*. 8 Oct. 2012. Web. <https://www.youtube.com/watch?v=8FD2NZ_affG0>.

8. Minnesota Historical Society. "Hinckley Fire of 1894." *Minnesota History Center*. 2 Feb. 2015. Web. <http://libguides.mnhs.org/hinckleyfire>.

9. Minnesota Historical Society.

10. "History of Hinckley Forest Fire." *Minnesota Geneology*. 2002. Web. <http://www.minnesotagenealogy.com/hinclkey-fire-history.htm>.

References

"The Great Hinckley Fire." *Rising Legion Films*. 8 Oct. 2012. Web. <https://www.youtube.com/watch?v=8FD2NZaffG0>.

"Great Hinckley Fire of 1894." *Hinckley.gov*. 18 Dec. 2014. Web. <http://www.hinckley.govoffice2.com/>.

Hinckley Fire Museum. 2014. Web. <http://hinckleyfiremuseum.com/index.html>.

"History of Hinckley Forest Fire." *Minnesota Genealogy*. 2002. Web. <http://www.minnesotagenealogy.com/hinckley-fire-history.htm>.

McNally, Janet. "The Hinckley Fire of 1894." *Tamaracklamb& wool*. 1997. Web. <http://www.tamaracksheep.com/Hinckley%20Fire.html>.

Minnesota Historical Society. "Hinckley Fire of 1894." *Minnesota History Center*. 2 Feb. 2015. Web. <http://libguides.mnhs.org/hinckleyfire>.

"On This Day in Weather History with Mark Mancuso: The Great Hinckley Fire (Saturday, September 1st, 1894)" *AccuWeather.com*. Web. <https://www.youtube.com/watch?v=z5Bzg4nztDk>.

About the Author

Dr. Vera E. Williams, Ph.D.

Vera Estelle Williams was born in Hawthorne, Wisconsin, on March 25, 1926. I attended a rural elementary school in Hawthorne and graduated from East High School, Superior, Wisconsin in 1944. After completing two years at Superior State Teacher's College, I transferred to La Crosse State Teacher's College, where I received a B.S. Ed. in 1948.

I worked my way through college as a railroad telegrapher on the Northern Pacific Railroad. For nearly ten years, between 1944 and 1956, I worked weekends, holidays, and summers for the railroad.

My physical education teaching experience includes all levels of public school education – elementary, secondary, college and university teaching. I taught at Portage, Wisconsin, 1948-1951; Sheboygan, Wisconsin, 1951-52; Superior, Wisconsin, 1952-53; Mt. Pleasant, Michigan, 1954-1961; and I came to Wisconsin State University, Oshkosh, Wisconsin in 1962, where I worked until I retired in 1988. I received my M.A. from the University of Michigan in 1954. I have done graduate work at Wayne State University, Michigan State University, Central Michigan University, and received my Ph.D. from Ohio State University in 1969.

Beloved Aunt Vera Passes Away

On May 25, 2016, a special express swooped down from the firmament and our beloved Aunt Vera took a one-way ticket to heaven.

Vera developed an arterial blood clot in her left foot in early March. The clot refused to dissolve, and she underwent extensive surgery. During her rehabilitation, Vera became septic. She peacefully slipped away with her loved ones at her side.

All who knew her will miss her greatly, but her stories and memories live on in this book that she lovingly shares with you.

Jill S. Williams Flateland

www.ingramcontent.com/pod-product-compliance
Lightning Source LLC
Chambersburg PA
CBHW042330150426
43194CB00001B/4